S9 *readiscover...*

Please return or renew this item by its due date to avoid fines. You will need your library card and PIN.

You can renew by:

- Phone
  0303 123 0035 (24 hour renewals)

- Online
  www.milton-keynes.gov.uk/libraries

or

- In person at any Milton Keynes Library

Milton Keynes Libraries

MILTON KEYNES
COUNCIL

D0235508

THE COURAGE OF COWARDS

THE UNTOLD STORIES OF FIRST WORLD WAR CONSCIENTIOUS OBJECTORS

by

Karyn Burnham

THE COURAGE
OF COWARDS

THE UNTOLD STORIES OF
FIRST WORLD WAR
CONSCIENTIOUS OBJECTORS

First published in 2014 by

an imprint of
Pen & Sword Books Ltd
47 Church Street
Barnsley
South Yorkshire
S70 2AS

ISBN:- 9781781592953

Printed and bound in the UK by CPI Group (UK) Ltd,
Croydon, CRO 4YY

Pen & Sword Books Ltd incorporates the imprints of Pen &
Sword Archaeology, Atlas, Aviation, Battleground, Discovery,
Family History, History, Maritime, Military, Naval, Politics,
Railways, Select, Social History, Transport, True Crime, and
Claymore Press, Frontline Books, Leo Cooper, Praetorian Press,
Remember When, Seaforth Publishing and Wharncliffe.

For a complete list of Pen & Sword titles please contact

PEN & SWORD BOOKS LIMITED

47 Church Street, Barnsley, South Yorkshire, S70 2AS, England
E-mail: enquiries@pen-and-sword.co.uk
Website: www.pen-and-sword.co.uk

For Pam

ACKNOWLEDGEMENTS

Thanks to Melvyn Kirby and Pamela Coleman of the British Library, without whom several obscure but invaluable books would have gone undiscovered. Jen Newby at Pen & Sword Books for her endless patience, enthusiasm and skilful editing. The staff at Leeds University Library, Liddle Collection for helping me get the best out of the archives and for untying the knotty problem of copyright. The Friends House Library and the Peace Pledge Union, both of whom provided information and photographs.

CONTENTS

The conscientious objector is a brave man. He will be remembered as one of the few noble actors in this world drama when the impartial historian of the future sums up the history of this awful war.

Siegfried Sassoon, 1917

INTRODUCTION

When choosing a title for this book, I was reluctant to use the word 'coward' in connection with conscientious objectors because, as I discovered in my research, these men were anything but cowards. However, the word cropped up wherever I looked because at the time that is how they were perceived: as cowards, shirkers, slackers, un-manly – the list goes on.

Contemporary propaganda posters presented a carefully crafted image of manhood defining 'real' men as those who fought for their families, for King and Country. Society was encouraged to reject and humiliate any able-bodied man not in uniform. Images of children asking their fathers, 'Daddy, what did YOU do in the Great War?', were designed to question a man's sense of self-worth and the now potent symbol of cowardice, the white feather, was routinely doled out to any man of fighting age seen outdoors in civilian clothing.

What also came across time and again, however, was the immense courage of these men. It is no easy route, standing up for your beliefs against a tidal wave of patriotism designed to belittle and crush your spirit; no soft option to be made to feel a worthless coward; and that was only the start of it. The men who found the courage to stand apart from the overwhelming majority, from society, and often from their own families, faced the kind of brutality normally reserved for the very worst kind of offenders. Locked in solitary confinement, they existed on bread and water rations, beaten and even condemned to death. Ironically, they were often punished more harshly than convicted murderers for refusing to commit exactly the same act, albeit under military orders.

Many COs chose some form of alternative service, like the Friends Ambulance Unit, frequently putting themselves in extreme personal danger to save the lives of others. No true coward could, or would, have willingly endured all of this; being a conscientious objector during the First World War was certainly no easy way out. I finally settled on the phrase 'The Courage of Cowards' as a way of challenging the old perception.

I also discovered that conscientious objectors were not an homogeneous group with similar backgrounds, education and outlook on life. Rather than mainly coming from affluent, well-educated families with a strong religious faith, many COs were working class and it was often strongly-held socialist principles that led them to object to the war. Sometimes isolated in their beliefs, they risked being censured by loved ones who, like the majority of the country, felt that refusing to fight was unpatriotic. I found stories of men, some of them still in their teens, being cut off by parents and siblings for refusing to fight, while other luckier men managed to retain the love and respect of family members who held opposing points of view.

The experiences re-told in *The Courage of Cowards* are just a small sample of many hundreds of stories, some well-documented, others less so and many inevitably lost forever. The majority of the stories that follow are drawn from the personal papers of the men concerned, unpublished memoirs, letters, diaries and interview transcripts from the Liddle Collection at Leeds University Library. The papers were full of so much more than just the bare facts of conscientious objection; they were filled with personality, humour, and such small personal details that I began to feel as though I had actually known some of the men involved. I wanted their voices to come through and their experiences to have the same emotional impact on the reader as they had on me, so I chose to adopt a fictional style to tell their stories. All the events, experiences, facts and dates are accurate and are easily corroborated by archives and official sources, including Hansard, because the treatment of conscientious objectors was discussed regularly in Parliament.

Through the research and writing of this book, I developed a greater understanding of the complex issues surrounding conscientious objection during the First World War and came to respect the men who were determined not to be forced into acting against their will; ordinary men who paid an extraordinary price in their fight for the principle of freedom.

Karyn Burnham, 2013

CHAPTER 1

THE OUTBREAK OF WAR

We are muddled into war.
(David Lloyd George)

When war broke out in the summer of 1914, it had not been long in the planning. Europe may have been a simmering pressure cooker of conflicting imperial agendas, but there was no lengthy political preamble; no bold declarations of intent or threats of invasion were made. When the spectre of war began to glare across the continent, it wasn't the result of cold, calculated strategy by any particular country. The catastrophe that was the First World War happened suddenly, unexpectedly, almost accidentally. War took hold of Europe while most people on the continent were enjoying their summer holidays.

When Archduke Franz Ferdinand, heir to the Austro-Hungarian throne, decided to make an official visit to Sarajevo, Bosnia at the end of June 1914, he had no idea of the extraordinary chain of events that would follow. Bosnia was part of the Austro-Hungarian empire and this inevitably caused political tensions with those who wanted to see Bosnia governed by Serbia. A group of students, supported by the nationalistic terrorist group The Black Hand, organised a protest against Austrian occupation and planned to attack the Archduke's entourage as it toured Sarajevo. One of these students, Gavrilo Princip, was successful in his attempt, assassinating both the Archduke and his wife as they

3

travelled through the streets in their open-topped car.

The Austro-Hungarian empire couldn't let the assassination of its heir pass without action, but didn't have either the army or the political leverage to take on Serbia alone. Instead, they turned to their old ally Germany for support and in the weeks that followed the Archduke's assassination, alliances were drawn, ultimatums were issued and brinkmanship was pushed to the limit. On 28 July, just one month after the assassination, Austria-Hungary declared war on Serbia prompting her ally Russia to mobilise troops, which in turn led Germany to declare war on Russia. By 1 August, Serbia and Austria were all but forgotten as the two mighty empires of Germany and Russia prepared for war.

Although Britain watched the escalating aggression with suspicion, wary of Germany's imperial might, the British Government was keen to reassure the public that it was under no obligation to engage in a European conflict. As of 1 August 1914, Britain had no intention of becoming embroiled in a war. On 3 August however, Germany declared war on France and mobilised troops to attack France's poorly defended borders with Belgium. This single action changed Britain's attitude to the conflict in Europe. Belgium was a neutral country and the ports of Ostend and Zeebrugge were vital for Britain's continental trade. Belgium's neutrality was protected by the 1839 Treaty of London, which stated that the 'guarantor countries [of which Britain was one] had the right to intervene in order to defend the neutrality of Belgium'. The Foreign Secretary, Sir Edward Grey, sent an ultimatum to the German Government to withdraw its troops from Belgium immediately or face a declaration of war from Britain.

Germany did not withdraw from Belgium and on 4 August 1914 Britain went to war with Germany to 'fulfil her obligations to Belgium and in defence of the rights of small nations'.

If the British Government was to declare war today, or announce the country's involvement in a conflict, our reaction as a nation may be mixed, but there would certainly be an overwhelming sense of apprehension for the future. Although there may be groups who feel that war is justified and unavoidable, for the majority a declaration of war is the worst possible news. It seems incredible, as a modern Briton, to consider the largely positive reaction to the declaration of war on 4 August 1914.

In response to Britain's ultimatum to Germany, excitement swept through the country and crowds gathered on the streets of London. As the evening wore on, crowds increased until Trafalgar Square, Parliament Square and Whitehall were a crush of bodies. *The Daily Mirror* reported that the King, Queen, Prince of Wales and Princess Mary had appeared on the balcony of Buckingham Palace at 8pm to the 'wild, enthusiastic cheers' of a 'record crowd'. As the 11pm deadline for Germany's response approached the crowds grew quiet, waiting for the chimes of Big Ben before erupting into cheering and shouting which, according to *The Times*, 'echoed...for nearly twenty minutes' before the King re-appeared on the balcony and the crowd began to sing the National Anthem.

This reaction was repeated throughout the country; factories sounded their sirens to inform workers that the country was at war and word was communicated to feverish gatherings in public places. Today, we associate scenes like this with events of national celebration, like a royal wedding or jubilee, never with something as malevolent as war. But then, people had no idea just how malevolent or long-lasting this new war was going to be. In August 1914, the war still seemed righteous, glamorous even. Britain was defending 'little Belgium' against the mighty imperial aggression of Germany. It seemed the honourable and morally right thing to do, to fulfil one's obligations, to help a friend in need.

During those early days of war, the newspapers adopted a largely patriotic stance. The *Daily Mirror* exclaimed: 'We could not stand aside! Britain will not allow Germany's fleet to batter France's undefended coast', and the *Daily Express* ran with the headline: 'England expects that every man will do his duty'. Even so, there were some dissenting voices: the *Manchester Guardian* warned that Britain faced 'the greatest calamity that anyone living has ever known', while the *Daily Herald*, under the editorship of prominent socialist George Lansbury, took an outright anti-war approach, running with headlines such as 'War is Hell'.

In the years prior to 1914, there had been a burgeoning pacifist movement supported by the likes of the Independent Labour

Party and the Trades Union Congress. On 2 August, a large peace demonstration took place in Trafalgar Square, addressed by Keir Hardy and George Lansbury among others. The gathered crowds wholeheartedly backed calls for Britain to stay out of the escalating hostilities in Europe. Two days later, with Britain committed to war, support for pacifism dwindled overnight and both the TUC and the Labour Party switched allegiance to support the government. Pacifism in Britain had been tolerated prior to the war, but from August 1914 it fast became seen as unpatriotic. The *Daily Herald* maintained its anti-war stance, despite plummeting sales and several of its contributors being imprisoned later in the war as conscientious objectors.

In practical terms, Britain was not prepared for war at such short notice. The British Army was comparatively small – one tenth the size of the German Army – so a massive injection of recruits was needed and quickly. The surge of patriotic fervour, the popular belief that it 'would all be over by Christmas' and, perhaps, a boyish desire for adventure prompted men to flock in their thousands to recruiting stations. In the first week of the war, 8,193 men joined up; 43,354 in the second, 63,000 in the third and an incredible 174,901 in the fourth week alone. Before the war was even one month old, almost 300,000 men had volunteered to fight for King and country. Secretary of State for War, Lord Kitchener believed that the war would last at least three years and was well aware that many more men would be needed. In the first week of September he began a recruitment campaign and by the end of the month the number of new recruits had risen to over 750,000.

Conscription wasn't introduced until 1916, so in those early stages of the war, no man was legally obliged to join up. Anyone joining the army did so voluntarily and it was the job of the recruitment campaign to persuade, cajole and coerce men into 'doing their bit'. Posters began to appear across the country, adorning walls, bulletin boards and hoardings with messages ranging from the direct (Kitchener's famous 'Your Country Needs You') to phrases which subtly pricked the conscience of any man not in uniform ('Surely you will fight for your King and Country? Come along boys, before it's too late') and the downright accusatory (John Bull pointing at the viewer, standing in front of a row of soldiers with gaps in the ranks asking – 'Who's absent? Is it you?').

Conscientious Objectors in Waiting

Until the introduction of the Military Service Act in January 1916, a man who objected to the war for any reason didn't have to do battle with the authorities because of his beliefs, he simply did not volunteer for the army. There may still have been a great deal of insidious social pressure and propaganda aimed at him but, fundamentally, he was free to live according to his conscience. Interestingly though, not all men who went on to become conscientious objectors felt that way at the beginning of the war.

Jack Foister was a 21-year-old student at Cambridge University when the war began. His father, a boat builder at Pembroke College, was a Congregationalist and his mother was Church of England, so Jack had had a strict Protestant upbringing yet oddly, this had left him free from any deep sense of faith. He attended church as and when he was supposed to, but that habit began to slip while he was at university. On the surface, Jack Foister was an easy-going young man with a mischievous sense of humour which made him popular with his peers.

A firm socialist, Jack could trace his political stance back to a specific event in his teenage years. He remembered reading the newspapers, aged about 15 or 16, and following with interest the reforms that the Liberal Chancellor of the Exchequer David Lloyd George was trying to pass through Parliament. Lloyd George had eventually introduced a whole host of welfare reforms, including pensions for the elderly, free school meals and state financial support for those unable to work. These reforms were to be funded by the 'People's Budget' of 1909, which increased taxes on the wealthy, although it met with heavy opposition from the Conservatives and was voted down in the House of Lords. Fired up by the seeming injustice of the Conservative Party's attitude, Jack attended a course on the history of socialism and the Labour Party run by prominent socialist Clifford Allen.

In August 1914 however, Jack was as wrapped up in the patriotic excitement as everyone else during the early days and he came very close to volunteering. It happened in the local park on a Sunday afternoon; as the warmth of the summer wore on, Jack sat on the grass with his friends Ernest and Tom, both of whom were fresh from the local recruiting office.

"I can't wait to get out there!" Tom said, rubbing his hands together with alacrity. "Help teach the Hun a lesson or two about bullying".

"Have you made up your mind yet?" Ernest asked, squinting at Jack against the sun.

"Not yet". Jack replied. "I've only got a year left at Cambridge, seems foolish to give up on my studies now when I've worked so hard".

"A year?!" Ernest said. "But it'll be all over by then. You'll miss it".

"Why pass up on the chance of adventure for the sake of your studies?" Tom chipped in. "It's something to tell your grandchildren, how you helped stop the Hun from taking over Europe. What were your plans for after university? Civil Service wasn't it? Not much opportunity for adventure then is there?"

"Well, I was thinking of the Indian Civil Service actually. Quite a bit of adventure to be had in India I would have thought". Jack said, a little defensively, and his friends laughed.

"But it's still the Civil Service!" Tom said. "Look, the war'll be over in no time, then you can go back to your studies and pick up where you left off. Cambridge'll still be there, it won't go anywhere while you're away".

"Well, it might if the Germans invade". Ernest said jokingly. "German scholars everywhere and no room for Jack. We have to stop them Jack, we simply have to!" Ernest exclaimed in a fine show of melodrama, clasping his hands together in a mock plea. The rest of the afternoon passed in a similar vein, with the band playing patriotic tunes and men in new military uniforms spending final hours with families or sweethearts, until Jack was convinced that he would indeed be foolish to miss such an opportunity and walked home with a spring of determination.

He found his parents in the front parlour; his father sucking on his pipe, engrossed in a book and his mother concentrating on a crossword in the newspaper.

"That was good timing Jack, I've just brewed some tea". His mother said, laying the paper aside and heading to the kitchen. In his enthusiasm, Jack didn't think to close the door after her before speaking to his father.

"I've come to a decision father, I've decided to enlist", he announced. There was an almighty clatter from the kitchen as his mother dropped a pan. The two men looked at one another and Jack's father shut the door before responding quietly.

"What's brought this on?"

"I've been in the park with Tom and Ernest; they've enlisted and almost every other man in the park was in uniform. It'd be wrong not to go and do my bit too".

After a thoughtful pause, Jack's father responded. "That's very laudable son; I'm proud of you". He patted Jack fondly on the back. "But what's the hurry? You only have a year left at Cambridge; well less than a year actually. Why not finish your studies and join up then?"

"Because it'll all be over by then. Everyone says so".

"I happen to think 'everyone' is wrong", his father said, shaking his head. "All this 'it'll be over by Christmas' nonsense is just bravado. There are too many countries involved, too many conflicting agendas. I think the war will still be raging away when you've finished your exams next year. And besides", he tapped out his pipe into the grate, "I'm in the Territorials and bound to get called up; your brother is likely to go soon too. Your mother can't stand losing everyone at once, she needs to know one of us is safe eh?"

So, after some thought, Jack Foister decided to continue at Cambridge and, assuming the war hadn't ended by then, he would join up after his final exams.

David Blelloch was 19 when war was declared and preparing to go to Oxford when the new academic year started in September. Despite winning a scholarship to St John's College in 1913, he had been unable to take up his place the previous year after contracting typhoid fever and taking almost eight months to recover. Like Jack Foister, David was a socialist and could also trace his political views to Lloyd George's welfare reforms and the 'People's Budget'. He recalls being shocked by attacks on Lloyd George in *The Daily Mail*, which had argued that giving money to the aged and infirm would divert valuable funding from the navy and therefore weaken Britain's ability to defend herself. The *Mail* demanded to be told whether Britain would 'surrender her maritime supremacy to provide old age pensions'. David remembered thinking: 'If that's Conservatism, I want nothing to do with it'.

David took an avid interest in the news, just like most people at that time; he read the newspapers voraciously and formed his own opinions about the war. He wasn't taken in by the propaganda or the call to arms, nor did he feel a particular swell of patriotism for King and country. He did, however, see that Germany and Austria were the aggressors in this conflict and came to the decision to apply for a commission in the army, rather than take up his place at Oxford. When he broke this news to his mother, there was a long silence. Mrs Blelloch bit her lip, trying to hold back the torrent of words that threatened to spill out and which she knew would do no good. Her son was a curly-haired, boyish youth who looked more like 16 than 19 and she had a habit of talking to him as though he were still a boy instead of the man he almost was.

"I don't think you are well enough to join the army", she said eventually.

"Pardon?" Of all the reactions he had expected from her, that was one he hadn't anticipated.

"You've barely recovered from the typhoid, you're not up to full strength yet, not by a long way".

"Nonsense!" he laughed. "I've never felt fitter!" Which wasn't strictly true.

"You may feel fit, but you're not". David began to shake his head. "I'm serious David! The army is very physical and what kind of conditions do you think you'd be living in? You'd be ill again in no time and what use would you be to the army then?"

David was irritated, but he had a nagging feeling that his mother might just have a point and he agreed to visit the family doctor before contacting the army. His mother's instinct was proved right and he was declared still far from fit enough for active service. Despite his frustration, David accepted that the army had no room for a sickly officer and took up his place at Oxford with a view to applying for a commission the following year, if the war wasn't over by then...

Charles Dingle was another example of a young man keen to enlist at the beginning of the war, only to later develop a pacifist stance. Born in Kingston, Jamaica, Charles was the son of a naval marine engineer. An intelligent boy, he had won a scholarship to Taunton School and a further scholarship to Hartley College (now Southampton University). A student in the Engineering Department of Hartley College, Charles was 16 when the war started.

The college was abuzz with excitement in those first few weeks; many students soon left to join the army and those that remained rattled around half-empty corridors and classrooms feeling like they were missing out on the chance of a great adventure. Charles, caught up in the thrill of it all, discussed the possibility of enlisting with his friends, but he was too young to join the army and knew he wouldn't fool anyone that he was over 19, which was the minimum age for service overseas.

A rapid change came over the country with breathtaking speed in those opening weeks of the war, particularly in the south where troops were gathering prior to embarkation. The countryside around Southampton, so familiar to Charles, soon became like an armed camp. Tents were pitched by the hundred and the towns and roads became clogged with khaki.

One evening after college, Charles and his friends Eddie and Arthur cycled down to the docks, getting as close as they were allowed, to watch the ordered, noisy chaos of embarkation. A constant stream of soldiers, horses, guns, munitions and vehicles were being marshalled on to vessels of varying sizes. It was a thrilling sight for a group of impressionable boys.

"Look at that!" Eddie said with a whistle, as the massive barrel of an artillery gun was winched high into the air.

"What do you think the range of that would be?" Charles wondered.

"Couple of miles at least", Eddie said with a shrug. "Can you imagine the sound of it?"

"Especially if there's more than one".

"I can't believe I'm going to miss out on all this!" Eddie groaned.

"I thought you were going to try and enlist?"

"I did". Eddie hung his head.

"And? What happened?"

"Well, I didn't get in, obviously", Eddie replied truculently. "The sergeant clapped me on the back and said: 'Nice try sonny, come back when you can grow whiskers'". Eddie mocked the sergeant's patronising tone.

Charles laughed and gave him a friendly shove. "Well, it was a bit of a long shot wasn't it? I'd have got the same treatment if I'd gone".

To the delight of Charles, Eddie and all the other engineering students, the college workshops were soon switched to making shells; finally some war-work the students could become involved in. In his memoirs, Charles remembers being excited about this, about playing a part in the overall scheme of things, because at that stage he still hadn't developed his 'pacifist scruples'.

Other men, however, believed that the war was wrong from the start. James Landers, for example, was 21 when the war began and had no intention of volunteering to join the army. James had endured a childhood worthy of a Dickens novel. Born into the slums of Salford, his alcoholic father died when James was 10 and subsequently it seems that his mother went through a succession of dubious sexual relationships and was often incapable of raising her children. Consequently, James had spent his formative years in and out of workhouses and the homes of various relatives, all of whom seemed to despise him and want rid of him as soon as possible.

Aged 14, James found a job as delivery boy for a local grocery shop owned by an overseer of the local branch of the Christian Brethren. His life became more stable and he began to understand a little of his mother's lifestyle, of 'sin's ugliness' and why he had been so bullied as a child. James loved his mother and vowed to stand by her, support her and keep her on the straight and narrow.

By the time he was 19, James had left the grocery shop and was working at the Peel Conner Telephone Works in Salford, where he began studying to become an electrician by correspondence course. James was determined to improve his lot in life and to leave behind the mire of poverty and sin that had been his childhood. He regularly attended the United Methodist Church, which he felt provided him with a clear path towards salvation. In August 1914, the question of whether to enlist or not was simple for James. The Bible says 'Thou Shalt Not Kill', and so therefore killing your fellow man is murder, even when flags are being waved around and national honour is supposed to be secured through it. James was determined to live peaceably according to the word of God and to secure the salvation of his aberrant mother.

Men of Britain! Will You Stand This?

In the summer of 1914, the war swept across Britain like a tsunami overturning all that was established and understood. Everything changed; nothing remained the same. The infrastructure of the country was changed; the railways and the roads saw their usage changed; the coastline was no longer a place for holidaying but a vulnerable border in need of defending; factories and offices lost workers and had their production changed. Perhaps most important of all, people and attitudes changed; particularly towards anyone living in Britain who had the misfortune of being German, of German descent or in possession of a vaguely Germanic-sounding name.

Prior to the war, the government had been in the process of dealing with what it termed the 'alien problem' by compiling a register of names of all non-naturalised British residents. In the opening days of the war, the passage of the Alien Restrictions Act through Parliament ensured that the government had the power to curtail the movements of 'aliens'. Further laws followed prohibiting them from sending letters abroad, owning wireless sets, cameras, firearms, motor cars – the list goes on. The government began arresting all non-naturalised German, Austrian and Hungarian males of military age and either repatriating or interning them. By the end of September 1914, there were 13,600 'enemy aliens' in internment camps throughout the country, 10,500 of whom were civilians.

As the months wore on, the government began to close down premises that were owned or frequented by 'aliens' and the suspicions of the establishment filtered down through every strata of society, until even the most innocent of German shopkeepers became seen as the enemy within. The *Daily Mail* demanded: 'Refuse to be served by a German Waiter' and Horatio Bottomley, the editor of *John Bull* magazine, went as far as calling for a vendetta against all Germans in Britain:

> *I call for a vendetta against every German in Britain, whether 'naturalised' or not. You cannot naturalise an unnatural beast – a human abortion – a hellish freak. But you can exterminate it. And now the time has come. No German must be allowed to live in our land.*

The hatred and suspicion of Germans in Britain was so strong that even someone in high office like the First Sea Lord, Prince Louis of Battenberg, son of a German prince and born in Austria, was hounded out of office, later changing his name to the more anglicised Mountbatten.

The initial swell of euphoria that had driven men into recruitment offices subsided and the patriotic surge to serve King and country in protection of 'little Belgium' passed. When news began to filter through of high numbers of casualties and battles lost, it became apparent that this war would last far beyond the much vaunted Christmas deadline. As the number of men willing to volunteer began to decline, so the number of men needed at the Front continued to increase. By the end of the year, the recruitment campaigns began to take a hard line, determined to shock, anger or plain manipulate men into volunteering.

One poster in early 1915 showed number 2 Wykeham Street, a terraced house in Scarborough destroyed by German bombardment in December 1914. In front of the wreckage and rubble stands a small girl holding a baby. Above the picture, the exhortation: 'MEN OF BRITAIN! WILL YOU STAND THIS?' and the words below the picture state the brutal facts: '78 Women and

Children were killed and 228 Women and Children were wounded by the German raiders. ENLIST NOW'. It became increasingly important to emphasise the threat and peril to British shores and to 'defenceless' women and children.

Other posters questioned a civilian man's masculinity, shaming him into action by showing a small girl sitting upon her father's knee, asking him: "Daddy, what did YOU do in the Great War?" Recruiters were paid a shilling for every man they recruited and as the volunteer numbers dwindled, so the recruiters began turning a blind eye to minor inconveniences like age, height and general health.

The first organised anti-military movements began as early as autumn 1914 with the formation of the No Conscription Fellowship, or NCF as it was popularly known. Fenner Brockway, a member of the Independent Labour Party, committed pacifist and editor of the ILP's newspaper, the *Labour Leader*, along with Clifford Allen, (who had been such an influence on the young Jack Foister) began the movement. In November, Brockway published an appeal inviting all young men who intended to refuse military service to join. There were just 300 members initially, plus men who were beyond military age, but all shared the NCF's pacifist agenda and were prepared to help and support the cause.

By the time 1914 drew to a close, the world was much altered and Britain was still adjusting to a war that would perpetuate far beyond initial expectations. The nation had lost its faith in a quick resolution and was not yet accustomed to the realities of modern, mechanised warfare. Thousands of men had already died on the battlefields and thousands more were needed.

CHAPTER 2

THE BEGINNING OF CONSCIENCE

Jack F.G. If you are not in khaki
by the 20th I shall cut you dead. Ethel M
(Personal column of *The Times*, **8 July 1915)**

The war did not hasten towards the hoped for conclusion during 1915. Instead, it continued to spread across Europe like ink spilled on to a map. Germany had advanced into French territory, occupying a tenth of her land and a third of her industrial capacity. Along the Western Front, 110 Allied divisions confronted 100 German divisions in France and Belgium; while 80 German and Austro-Hungarian divisions stood fast against 83 Russian divisions along an Eastern Front stretching from the Baltic Sea in the North to the Carpathian Mountains in the South.

The Eastern Front was more than twice the length of the Western Front and inadequate troop numbers allowed Germany to push Russia out of Poland, eventually taking Warsaw on 4 August. In an attempt to divert, and therefore weaken, the German Army in the West, First Lord of the Admiralty Winston Churchill organised an amphibious attack on the Dardanelles and Gallipoli in Turkey. The plan failed and Allied troops found themselves under Turkish siege. Despite several Allied offensives, no real progress was made and the troops were finally evacuated in December 1915.

The scale of the war had increased so rapidly that there wasn't enough time to adequately train the thousands of volunteers pouring into recruiting offices. The experienced, professional soldiers of the pre-war regular army were all too few and were being lost in battle at an alarming rate. The need to get men into uniform and to the Front quickly was becoming increasingly disproportionate to the length of time required to train and equip them. The nature of warfare was also evolving in terms of mechanisation and artillery and on 22 April 1915 poison gas was used as a weapon for the first time by the Germans at Ypres. Ironically, the German Army was not prepared for the success of that first gas attack and failed to exploit the four-mile gap which opened up in the Allied Front Line.

Meanwhile, on the Home Front, every suitable factory, plant and production line was being given over to war work. In the beginning, the transition from peacetime engineering work to the manufacture of wartime munitions was hasty and poorly planned, with over-optimistic production targets and finished goods of varying quality and reliability. A lack of artillery shells was blamed for the failure at Aubers Ridge on 9 May 1915 and the loss of 11,600 lives – a crisis which contributed to the formation of the Ministry of Munitions. As Munitions Minister, David Lloyd George ensured a cohesive alliance between government and businesses. By the end of the war, the Ministry employed around three million workers in 20,000 factories.

On 19 January 1915, Britain suffered its first air raid casualties when two Zeppelins dropped bombs on Great Yarmouth and King's Lynn. At about 8.30pm, 53-year-old Sam Smith of Great Yarmouth left his workshop to find out what all the noise was about. A bomb hit a house on the opposite side of the road and a piece of shrapnel caught Sam in the head, killing him instantly. Rumour had it that the Zeppelins had been deliberately guided in by the headlights of two cars on the coastal roads driven by non-naturalised Germans, or 'enemy aliens'. The rumours were investigated and found to be thoroughly unsubstantiated.

Although the death toll from these first Zeppelin raids was small (only three people were killed), the damage to morale was severe as, for the first time, Britons felt vulnerable in their own homes. Zeppelin raids continued throughout the war, becoming a regular occurrence along the East Coast and in London. Air raids were heralded, not by sirens as in the Second World War, but by whistles blown by policemen or even boy scouts and although official instructions were to go indoors and shelter under a table, such was the fascination with the enormous airships that people often stood outside and watched them fly over.

In the opening months of 1915, Britain underwent a familiarisation process with the war; a settling-in to a new, less predictable way of living. The demographic shifted as men went to fight and women went to work; businesses swapped production from pots and pans to guns and bullets; and trade, both into and out of Britain, became a complex, perilous affair. People adjusted their expectations of life; they grew used to being apart from loved ones, grew used to straitened times and grew increasingly intolerant of those who were different and those who were perceived as not doing their bit.

Recruitment campaigns and propaganda began to broaden their approach. Instead of concentrating solely on a direct appeal to young men, they also brought pressure to bear by more indirect methods: attempting to emasculate men through their womenfolk. One bold poster exclaimed: 'WOMEN OF BRITAIN SAY – "GO!"' and depicted a mother, a wife and a young child watching with anxious pride as soldiers march off to war. Another notice enquired 'Is your "Best Boy" wearing Khaki?' and went on to ask: 'If he does not think that you and your country are worth fighting for – do you think he is WORTHY of you?' The notice advises women 'not to pity the girl who is alone', because 'her young man is probably a soldier – fighting for her and her country – and for YOU', before warning the poor young woman that if her young man neglects his duty, the time will come when he neglects her too.

Some pamphlets were even more explicit, like the one addressed to 'MOTHERS!' and 'SWEETHEARTS!' reminding women of the monstrous attacks on Belgian civilians. It warned them: 'If you cannot persuade him to answer his Country's Call and protect you now *Discharge him as unfit!*' The general public were being whipped into a patriotic frenzy where any man out of uniform was viewed as a shirker, a slacker and a coward. So powerful were the messages given out by the authorities and the press, that people became blind to any fact other than the lack of uniform.

One of the most infamous and potent icons of 'cowardice' during the war was the white feather. Its symbolism lives on even now, although the intervening years have given us perspective and sympathy for the men unlucky enough to receive them. The white feather as a symbol of cowardice has its origins in cockfighting, where a white feather appearing in the tail of a cockerel indicated an inferior cross-breed and a poor fighter.

The issuing of a white feather to someone accused of cowardice entered popular culture via the likes of A.E.W. Mason's 1902 novel *The Four Feathers* and P.G. Wodehouse's 1907 work *The White Feather*. In *The Four Feathers*, the protagonist Harry Faversham resigns his commission to avoid being sent to Egypt; his cowardice is rewarded by the issuing of four white feathers, one each from three of his peers and the fourth from his disappointed fiancée; Faversham sets about regaining both reputation and fiancée by travelling to Egypt, where he is eventually hailed a hero. In Wodehouse's *The White Feather*, schoolboy Sheen walks away from a fight and is ostracised by his school friends; in order to win back the respect of his friends and the honour of his school, Sheen takes secret boxing lessons.

The issuing of white feathers during the First World War started on a small scale in August 1914, when Vice Admiral Penrose-Fitzgerald banded together a group of 30 young women in his hometown of Folkestone and prompted them to give a white feather to any young man not in uniform. The practice was reported in the press and spread across the country in a matter of months. After the war, the writer Virginia Woolf all but dismissed the white feather campaign, arguing that in reality there had only been perhaps 50 or 60 feathers issued. Judging by the scores of first-hand accounts recorded during the intervening century, it seems likely that this was a gross underestimate.

White feathers were doled out all over the country and by women of all ages. Their motives varied, sometimes the feather was a genuine expression of frustration at seeing young men idling at home while their own husband, sweetheart, or son was fighting. Often though, a white feather was issued out of sheer malice by young women looking for mischief. This usually happened in cities, where there was a certain degree of anonymity.

Girls would go out in twos or threes with the sole intention of hunting down a man out of uniform and humiliating him on the street. They chose their prey indiscriminately and sometimes got it terribly wrong.

Corporal J.P. Cope was home on leave and taking his wife out for tea in a cafe, when three young women approached their table and thrust three white feathers into his hand. Unaware of their meaning, Cope showed his wife, who was understandably furious. She followed the women and demanded to know what they were about. "He should be in khaki in France" one of the women said, to which Mrs Cope retorted that they "should be in a munitions factory making ammunitions for the soldiers to defend themselves". Mrs Cope insisted they return the following day; this time her husband was in full uniform. The three women apologised and offered to buy them tea, an offer which Mrs Cope refused on the grounds that the 'in-sightless' [sic] women had no idea what her husband had gone through in the first year of the war.

Gunner Frederick Broom was only 15 years old, but had somehow managed to persuade the army that he was 19. He was involved in the retreat from Mons, the Battle of the Marne and the advance to Ypres, before he contracted enteric fever and was invalided back to England. He was still only 16. Crossing Putney Bridge one day, Frederick was accosted by four girls and given three white feathers. Frederick told them his story, but they wouldn't believe him and a small crowd gathered to watch Frederick defend himself against the giggling girls. He felt so humiliated that he walked away from the group, straight into the offices of the 37th London Territorial Association of the Royal Field Artillery and rejoined the army.

Occasionally, the thoughtless actions of these women had truly tragic consequences. James Cutmore, a married man with three young daughters, had tried to volunteer in 1914 but was rejected because of his poor eyesight. Walking home from work one evening in 1916, he was approached by a young woman who pushed a white feather onto him and called him a shirker. James enlisted the next day; poor eyesight did not matter quite so much by that stage of the war. The last time he was home on leave, James

21

was so badly affected by shell shock that he barely spoke a word. Rifleman Cutmore died of wounds at the Front on 28 March 1918.

Despite encouraging women to push their menfolk to enlist by whatever means possible, the authorities were surprisingly shocked when the white feather campaign was put into practice. Major Leonard Darwin, the son of Charles Darwin, delivered a lecture to the Women's League of Honour entitled 'On the Meaning of Honour', both encouraging women to pressure their men to war and censuring them for the issuing of white feathers, which he said "require[d] no courage on the woman's part, but merely a complete absence of modesty". The writer and recruiting officer Coulson Kernahan, usually keen on any method of recruitment, believed that white feathers were often issued out of rancour, not towards the men themselves, but to the women who were lucky enough to still have their loved ones at home. Kernahan told women that the issuing of white feathers "far from witnessing to your patriotism, is witness only to the fact that you are unpardonably ignorant, vulgar and impertinent".

As 1915 wore on and the lists of killed and wounded grew ever longer, so the call for the introduction of conscription gathered voice. Liberal Prime Minister Asquith, along with the Labour Party and the Trade Unions, was against the very idea of conscription but Asquith found himself under increasing pressure from the influential, largely Tory, pro-conscriptionist movement. The final blow for Asquith came in September when, despite the foundation of the Ministry of Munitions in May, the shortage of shells at the disastrous Battle of Loos contributed to the loss of 16,000 lives, with another 25,000 wounded. In order to survive politically, Asquith had no option but to form a coalition with the Conservative and Labour parties and this gave the Conservatives the chance to argue for conscription from within government.

The first step towards conscription had come in July in the form of a National Registration Scheme, a type of census which recorded the occupations of men and women between the ages of 15 and 65. The information gathered under this scheme showed that there were around 1.8 million men of fighting age who were neither enlisted nor involved in vital 'war work'. The scheme played right into the hands of the pro-conscriptionists and Lord Northcliffe, owner of both *The Times* and *Daily Mail*, used the findings to demand, via his newspapers, that these 'slackers' be forced to serve.

In October, the next step on the fraught path towards conscription was introduced; the Derby Scheme (named after the Director-General of Recruiting, Lord Derby), 'encouraged' men of fighting age to 'attest' that they were willing to serve their country should they be required to do so. Men who attested were given armbands to wear, which marked them out from the 'slackers' and to some degree, protected them from the shame of the white feather.

Meanwhile Fenner Brockway, Clifford Allen and the No Conscription Fellowship were concentrating all their resources into opposing conscription. The NCF had moved from its humble beginnings in Brockway's Derbyshire home to offices in Merton House, Salisbury Court in Fleet Street. As conscription became increasingly likely, so membership of the NCF grew and a network of local branches were established throughout the country; those who joined the NCF declared their resolution not to undertake military service should conscription be introduced.

THE SHAPING OF CONSCIENCE

Upon taking his place at Oxford University in 1914, David Blelloch found that, rather than having to explain his socialist views, he was among students who both understood and shared his position. He attended debates long into the night about the injustice of war; of the 'powers that be' pitching working class men and women who had no gripe with one another into a fight to the death.

"How is it possible for a greengrocer say, or a labourer in some small town in Germany, to have any kind of grievance with a shopkeeper or a gardener in...St Albans for example?" David's friend Joseph Kaye said. "They are just ordinary men, working to provide a living for their families. They both want fundamentally the same thing, whichever country they live in, and yet they are being forced to blow one another to pieces with guns and bombs. It's immoral, plain and simple".

Leaning back in his chair, Joseph inhaled deeply on a cigarette pinched between forefinger and thumb. "And what's more", he added, squinting at his friends through wisps of blue-grey smoke, "the working man on either side will gain nothing from this war, whatever the outcome. Every country involved will be bankrupt by the end of it and who will suffer? Not the men in power, that's for sure".

"You know, if you look at how much Britain has spent on this war already", David added, wiping the froth of his beer from his top lip, "it's enough to provide every family in this country with a decent house and a piece of land. Why can the government find money to fund a war, but not to provide a reasonable standard of living for its citizens? It's no better than social control".

David liked and respected Joseph Kaye, who validated his previously amorphous socialism. Under the guidance of Joseph's friendship, David's views matured and his confidence grew. He no longer felt the urge to 'do his bit' for a cause he didn't actually believe in and was thankful for the family doctor's insistence on his unfitness for the army.

Joseph was particularly influential among his circle at Oxford because of his background: he was of German-Jewish descent. Although Joseph had been born in England, his father was German and, until 1914, the family name had been Kaufman. Joseph's father had changed his name when it became obvious that anyone with German connections was in for a rough ride. Because of his family background, Joseph was able to dispel the myths of propaganda surrounding 'the evil Hun' and portray the lives of ordinary Germans as being comparable to those of ordinary Britons.

Determined to play a part in the fight against conscription, Joseph and David joined the NCF and became secretaries for the Oxford branch; they organised meetings, distributed leaflets and pamphlets and offered advice to those who wanted to object to enlistment on conscientious grounds. Unfortunately, someone with strong pacifist views and the charisma to express them eloquently could only go unnoticed for so long in a society geared towards patriotism. The regular packages of socialist and pacifist pamphlets being delivered to Joseph's lodgings had attracted the attention of the authorities, who considered the material seditious and began to take a keen interest in his activities.

One afternoon, both David and Joseph were distributing NCF leaflets outside a local recruiting office, an exercise that was bound to get them noticed. Joseph, however, was not content with doling out leaflets to passers-by; he was a talented orator and took every opportunity to air his views. On this particular occasion, he had attracted a sizeable, and not wholly unsympathetic crowd, and was well and truly into his stride.

"You cannot believe the lies being told by the Press about ordinary German people for they are being told the same lies about you. It benefits governments for us to believe these lies, it fires us up, angers us, encourages us to fight...for what? Our freedom? We had our freedom before this war started but we have less freedom already and if the Government introduces conscription then you", he pointed at a young man at the front of the crowd, "and you and you...and thousands like you will have no freedom at all. Regardless of your circumstance, your beliefs, your families. You will have no choice but to face men just like you; to fight them, to kill them and to be killed by them. What a waste! What a waste of human life, of talent and of the future!"

He paused, looking over the crowd, reading faces, seeing heads nodding in agreement. "Don't let them do it! Don't let them make you part of this obscene capitalist mechanism called war! You *do* have a right to freedom; freedom to choose; freedom to insist on your right to live peaceably –"

"Alright! That's enough!" A voice cut across him, loud and authoritative. David, who had been handing out leaflets to the crowd, spun round and saw three policemen pushing their way to the front. The one who had spoken took hold of Joseph's arm and pulled him down off the small stool he was standing on to address the crowd.

"I'm entitled to express my views!" Joseph said, trying to pull his arm free from the constable.

"Not when those views are seditious and unpatriotic you're not, sonny. What's your name anyway?"

"That's none of your business", Joseph replied, as his other arm was taken by a second constable. "Let me go! This is outrageous!"

"It most certainly *is* our business *Mr Kaufman,*" the third policeman, a sergeant, said. Joseph stopped struggling and his face went pale. David, realising the seriousness of the situation, pushed his way to the front of the already dwindling crowd.

"My name is *Kaye.* Joseph Kaye".

"Of course it is *now*. How else were you going to blend in and spread your seditious German lies?" The sergeant continued "Joseph Kaufman, you are under arrest on suspicion of being a German spy".

"Of course he's not a German spy!" David shouted. "He was born here like you and I!"

The sergeant turned to David and looked him up and down, noting the pile of pamphlets in his hand.

"Who are you?"

"A friend of Mr Kaye".

"Name?"

"None of your business", David answered with a bravado he didn't really feel.

"Name!" the sergeant growled.

"David Blelloch".

"Blelloch?" He frowned. "What kind of name is Blelloch? Sounds German to me."

"It's Scottish!"

"You don't sound Scottish".

"Well I certainly don't sound German!"

"You would say that, wouldn't you?" The sergeant took hold of David's arm. "You're also under arrest on suspicion of being a German spy". Both men were led away, bewildered and protesting their innocence. After some rudimentary checks into David's family background, it became obvious that he was British through and through, and he was released with a caution against becoming involved with undesirables. Joseph Kaye wasn't so fortunate; his German heritage and socialist views marked him out as a troublemaker and even though the police couldn't link him to anything genuinely subversive, he was imprisoned for two months.

***

It wasn't socialism that pricked the conscience of Charles Dingle however, it was his Christian faith. Both of Charles's parents were committed Christians and they had passed on the habit of regular church attendance to their son. While at college in Southampton, Charles attended the local Baptist church and was influenced by the minister, a Welshman by the name of John Morris. The theme of the Reverend Morris's sermons was that the pursuit of war was incompatible with Christianity and to Charles this made perfect sense. He was surprised to find that others in the congregation felt differently.

Determined to fully understand and clarify his own beliefs, Charles worked on a paper entitled 'Can There Be A Holy War?' which he presented to the Young People's Society at his church. After much debate and discussion with other members of the society, Charles came to the conclusion that there could be no such thing as a justifiable, holy war. By the summer of 1915, Charles had already decided he would not volunteer for the army and if conscription should be introduced; his conscience would forbid him from complicity.

He expected to be in for a rough ride from his father who, despite his religious faith, believed that the war was justified and that everyone should play their part. Charles's father was serving with the navy and was away at sea for long periods, so it was some months before Charles had the opportunity to discuss the issue with him. When Charles turned 18 in the autumn of 1915, however, he knew his father would expect him to join up voluntarily and it was only a matter of time before he would have to explain himself. His mother on the other hand, was sympathetic and supportive of Charles's pacifist views and in December 1915 she encouraged Charles to write to his father, explaining everything.

"It'll be much easier to express yourself by letter than face to face," she said, "and it'll give your father time to take it all in before he reacts".

"Time to calm down before he comes home you mean", Charles said resignedly as he sat down to begin writing the difficult letter.

His father's reply arrived in January 1916; he was furious and told Charles he must enlist at the earliest opportunity or he was 'nothing more than a coward'. Charles winced as he read this and blanched at the final line, which read: 'you must either obey me in this matter, or leave home and look after yourself'.

When his mother found him, Charles was sitting at the kitchen table, head in hands, fingers clenched in his thick, dark hair and the letter in front of him.

"Is that from you father?" she asked tentatively and Charles nodded. "May I read it?" He nodded again. After a few silent moments, she put the letter back on the table.

"Oh dear".

"I'm not a coward mum; really I'm not", Charles said with a sob in his voice.

"I know you're not and so does your father really. He's just angry, that's all. You know how he can be. It must be difficult for him to see your point of view when the war affects him every day".

"He says he'll throw me out if I don't enlist"

"Yes, well. Like I said, you know how he can be when he's angry. I'm sure it won't come to that".

When Charles heard that his father would be home on leave in February, he couldn't face the thought of an outright confrontation, so, in a bid to satisfy his father without compromising his own principles, Charles tried to join the Royal Army Medical Corps (RAMC), but his application was unsuccessful. There seemed no other alternative but to try to explain his position and hope that his father would understand.

Charles's father had been home for 24 hours before he brought the subject up. It was late afternoon and they were sitting at the kitchen table, playing chess in the failing winter light.

"I assume you've got all that conchie nonsense out of your system now they've brought conscription in?" His father asked casually as he took his son's knight.

Charles cleared his throat and embarked on a much rehearsed defence of his stance but only got as far as "...and Reverend Morris says – "

"Oh Reverend Morris this, Reverend Morris that!" His father exploded. "I'd like to meet this Reverend Morris and give him a piece of my mind! How dare he stand in the pulpit preaching pacifist nonsense in the name of Christianity? What does he know of warfare eh? And what do you know either for that matter? I'm out there", he jabbed his finger at some place over his shoulder, "defending King, country and everything you hold dear; seeing men die in defence of this country and you think you are in a position to make some high and mighty decision about the rights and wrongs of war? You arrogant young pup!"

"It's not like that dad! The Bible teaches that it's wrong to kill and – "

"I know full well what the Bible says boy! What do you suggest we do? Sit back and let the Hun rampage through Europe? Killing innocent women and children along the way? Hmm? Because that's what's been happening in Belgium. You're happy to sit back and let that carry on are you? For the sake of some juvenile idealism?"

"Dad, that's not fair! Of course I'm not happy to let it happen! The war is obscene, it's wrong and I will not play any part in prolonging it!" Charles shouted at his father for the first time in his life.

Banging his fist on the table and upsetting the chess pieces, his father stood up, tipping his chair over as he did so. "Quite happy to go to war with me though, I see?" he roared. "Conscientious objection? It's nothing more than base cowardice and I will not have a coward under my roof, not when good men are dying to keep you safe!"

Charles's mother burst into the room, unable to keep out of it any longer. "That's enough! Both of you!" She shouted. "Unless you want half the street to know our business?"

Her husband glared at her, but lowered his voice none the less. "I mean it!" he growled, "I will not tolerate a conchie coward in my house. If the boy wants to hold those kind of ideas, he can do it elsewhere. I want nothing more to do with him". He turned back to Charles. "You can pack your bags and get out today".

"But where will I go?" Charles felt suddenly sick.

"To hell for all I care". His father grabbed his jacket from the back of the fallen chair and stalked out.

"I'll talk to him", his mother said, stricken.

She did talk to him, but he was utterly uncompromising. In the end, she resorted to dragging out a few home truths about their marriage and his shortcomings as a husband over the years. The best result she could achieve was that Charles could remain at home until he had finished college and could support himself, but he would need to make alternative living arrangements whenever his father was home on leave. She also promised not to talk about Charles or even mention his name to her husband. It was a deeply unhappy situation, but at least Charles still had a roof over his head.

James Landers had no such issues with his parents; his father had died long ago and his mother relied upon the income he brought into the house. She had no desire for him to leave home and equally James had no desire to abandon her to the temptations of sin; he was determined to keep her on a righteous path. James, like Charles Dingle, was a deeply religious young man, though he took life seriously and had little time for frivolity. He worked as a lathe hand at the Peel Conner Telephone Works in Salford and spent his spare time studying a correspondence course to improve his job prospects and the Bible to improve his soul.

For James, the issue of whether to enlist or to yield to conscription was simple; wherever he looked in the Bible the message came back loud and clear: to kill another human being is wrong, it is a sin. James resolved to 'obey God and honour the King, with the conviction never in the reverse order'. Throughout 1915, James became more conscious of 'the fear of God and a desire to please and be directed by God'. In the summer of that year, under the guidance of his former employer, he attended an open baptism into the Christian Brethren, where he began to immerse himself wholeheartedly into studying the Bible, the Word and the voice of God.

James was popular enough with his workmates because he was good-natured and hard-working, but he wasn't the kind of man you'd invite down to the pub for a pint after work unless you wanted to end up arguing about scripture. One of his workmates, a man in his fifties by the name of Bill Hardy, could often be found arguing furiously with James over opposing interpretations of the Bible. Bill liked to think of himself as a 'regular' Christian; he attended church on Sundays, showed proper respect where it was due and believed that the war was justified and every man should be out there doing his bit. James's 'Bible thumping' attitude to Christianity inflamed Bill, who felt that James was wilfully misinterpreting the Bible to satisfy his own needs.

"Joined up yet?" Bill said. It was his regular way of greeting James at the start of a shift. Sometimes James would let it pass without comment, but if he was in the right frame of mind, he'd take Bill on and the whole shift would develop into a debate which invariably spilled into argument.

"I don't see how a man who believes in God as you claim to do – " James started to say, an hour into the exchange.

"I don't *claim* to believe in God sonny Jim, I *do* believe in God", Bill interrupted.

"Well then you know that God is all loving and all knowing, so when He says 'Thou Shalt Not Kill', it is not for us to question Him. It's our duty to obey Him. You're arguing for precisely the kind of disobedience of His word that led us into this war".

Bill was beginning to turn red; James's righteous, calm certainty got to him every time.

"What about God being all powerful too then?" Bill shouted now, partly to make himself heard over the noise of the lathe that James had just switched on. "If he was all powerful, he would have never let the war happen in the first place!"

James looked at him thoughtfully, almost placidly before replying. "You seem to be arguing against the existence of God at all. Just the kind of ill-informed argument I'd expect from an infidel".

"Don't call me an infidel! You f –"

"That's enough of that!" Their shift leader clapped Bill heartily on the back. "Give it a rest, both of you! You're drowning out the sound of the machinery for God's sake. And don't even think of making a comment about taking the Lord's name in vain". He looked at James. "You're paid to work, you can do your arguing in your own time".

With the threat of conscription looming, James thought long and hard about his options. Joining the army would be wholly against his convictions; refusing to join would likely land him in prison.

He wasn't afraid of prison, but it would mean he had no income and no means of supporting his mother. It was a stark choice: go against everything he believed in to earn a wage to support his mother, or stand up for his beliefs and leave her to fend for herself, the consequences of which didn't bear thinking of. He knew the Lord was testing him and knew he would somehow find a way of proving himself worthy.

There were thousands of young men in similar positions to David, Charles and James in 1915. Aware that conscription was likely to be introduced, they battled with their consciences, their families and their friends. Knowing that they would be perceived as lowly cowards, gaining little sympathy or understanding from the rest of the country, they struggled to come to a decision that would allow them to live honestly.

None of them could fully appreciate what the next few years held in store for them, nor how their consciences and their courage would be tested to the limit.

CHAPTER 3

THE MILITARY SERVICE ACT

Every...man on Thursday, March 2nd 1916, will be
deemed to have enlisted for the period of the War
(An Outline of the Military Service Act, January 1916)

On 27 January 1916 the Military Service Act became law in Britain. The Act applied to every unmarried man over the age of 18 but under 41 and laid out eight classes of men who were exempt from conscription into the army: those who were not British citizens; members of the regular or reserve forces; men in the Royal Navy or Royal Marines; clergymen, priests or ministers; men who had been discharged from the Forces on grounds of ill-health; time-expired men from the army or navy; men who had tried to enlist but had been rejected; and finally, men who held a certificate of exemption. Any man who did not fit into one of these classes was 'deemed to have enlisted for the period of the War' as of Thursday, 2 March 1916.

When Prime Minister Asquith rose to introduce the Military Service Bill to the House of Commons on 5 January 1916, he did so with a heavy heart. Fundamentally against the principle of conscription, Asquith was ultimately left with no other choice. He was under political pressure from his Conservative coalition partners, as well as facing the stark reality that the numbers of men being lost in battle could no longer be replenished by volunteers alone. Referring to, and relying heavily upon, the Derby Report to support his arguments, Asquith set about presenting the Military

Service Bill to the House.

The Derby Report summarised the results of the previous year's National Registration Scheme and subsequent attestation of men under the Derby Scheme. Broadly speaking, the Derby Report claimed that if one were to subtract the number of men who had 'attested' (declared) their intent to serve from the number of British men of military age, there was a surplus of around 650,000 men. These were men, the report argued, who were able to fight, but had no intention of enlisting of their own free will.

The validity of these figures was hotly disputed by opponents of conscription, particularly Sir John Simon, who had recently resigned as Home Secretary over the issue. Simon argued that the figure of 650,000 was arbitrary and included several classes of men who were either unfit for, or excluded from, military service. Despite Simon's incisive demolition of Derby's statistics, the report still underpinned the arguments in support of the Bill, with Asquith arguing that it merely represented 'the redemption of the promise' given by those who had attested under Lord Derby's scheme.

Asquith managed to avoid compromising his principles over conscription completely, however. The first draft of the Bill had allowed for three classes of exemption from military service; first: employment in work 'expedient to the National interests'; second: if becoming a soldier would cause serious financial hardship to the man's family and third: ill-health or infirmity. The Bill presented by Asquith on 5 January was the second draft and had a crucial fourth clause, which read:

> That he has a conscientious objection to combatant service. The certificate of exemption may be from combatant service only, in which case the man would not be exempt from service in a non-combatant unit, such as the Army Medical Corps. It may be made a condition of his exemption that the applicant is, or will be, engaged in work which in the opinion of the Local Tribunal is of national importance.

This clause met with derision from the House, incredulous that the Bill would allow a man to escape military service purely on the grounds of conscience. Asquith stood firm and the Bill was passed a few weeks later by 383 votes to 36.

It was the responsibility of each individual to raise his objection, conscientious or otherwise, to military service and the duty of local tribunals to reach a decision over exemption. The tribunals were comprised of between five and ten people; usually 'upstanding' members of the community and almost always men. In addition, a military representative was present to ensure that no one got off lightly. The job of the tribunal was to assess the validity of each man's claim, but as around 750,000 men applied for some form of exemption between January and July 1916, the sheer weight of cases meant that tribunals had little time or patience when considering the validity of a conscientious objection. Many conscientious objections were refused outright at local tribunal, some were granted exemption from combatant service upon appeal, but only around 350 were granted total exemption by the time the war ended.

With the threat of the Military Service Act looming, membership of the No Conscription Fellowship increased. In April 1916, the organisation held a national convention in London attended by 2,000 members, many of whom were already awaiting arrest for failing to report for duty after being called up. The NCF hoped that if enough men objected to compulsory military service, then the system would grind to a halt and the Military Service Act could be overturned. The convention was a fraught affair; Clifford Allen, chairman and co-founder of the NCF, warned police that he expected trouble. There were noisy protests outside the Friends Meeting House in Bishopsgate as serving soldiers and the general public harangued members as they arrived.

So volatile were opinions of the NCF and conscientious objectors that there are conflicting reports on just how difficult attending the convention was. Fenner Brockway recalls several sailors climbing over the railings only to be greeted by handshakes and offers of tea, whereas the press variously reported the sailors being thrown out 'collarless and bleeding' or not managing to enter the hall at all. Once the convention was underway, delegates were asked to refrain from cheering or applauding for fear it would inflame the crowd outside; instead they were asked to show appreciation by waving their handkerchiefs. By the end of the convention a resolution had been reached to oppose any form of alternative service that would support the continuance of the war.

Facing up to the reality of conscription and tribunals, the NCF directed a lot of its resources to supporting and advising men facing tribunal hearings. Fenner Brockway, along with six fellow members, produced the pamphlet *Why I am a Conscientious Objector*. The pamphlet listed the types of questions likely to be asked at tribunal, stated the position and beliefs of each contributor and laid out their detailed responses to each question. So for example, in answer to the question 'What particular kinds of National Service would you be willing to undertake?' Fenner Brockway answers: 'To me war is murder. If I consented to bargain with it I should feel I were guilty of participating in murder'. Other sample answers to this question carried the same message – National Service of any kind supported the war and was, therefore, out of the question.

PUTTING CONSCIENCES TO THE TEST

Jack Foister, 22, Teacher from Peterborough

By the time conscription was introduced, Jack Foister had left Cambridge with a good degree and was working as a teacher at a school in Peterborough. His final year at university had coincided with the first year of the war and his experiences were similar to those of David Blelloch. Jack's socialist views were shared by many of his peers and when Clifford Allen, who had been so influential in the formation of Jack's political opinions, co-founded the No Conscription Fellowship, Jack immediately joined.

Jack's father was a member of the Territorial Army and had been called up; as he was too old for overseas service, he was engaged in support work in Britain. Jack's mother, on the other hand, was very much against the war and supported his opinions although, out of respect for his father, they both avoided airing their views when he was home on leave.

Within a year of taking up his teaching post, Jack received his call up papers ordering him to report for service on 23 May 1916. He had already decided that he would not fight and had no intention of responding to the call up. His headmaster was sympathetic to Jack's cause and also reluctant to lose yet another member of staff at a time when recruiting new teachers was difficult enough. On a warm, promising morning in early April, the headmaster called Jack into his office to discuss the situation.

"Have a seat", said the headmaster, indicating the chair across the desk from him. Jack sat down and nervously pushed his spectacles back up onto the bridge of his nose; the head teacher was a portly, cheerful man whom Jack liked and respected but he wasn't entirely sure what the purpose of this meeting was.

"So what are we going to do about this call up of yours then?" the head began. "You're set on not fighting, yes?"

"Yes, sir. I've made no secret of my beliefs with regard to the war".

"Hmm. Well, I don't want to lose you from the teaching staff either. You're well qualified, a personable chap and the boys seem to like you. The question is, how are we going to handle it?"

"I will apply for exemption on grounds of conscience".

"Hmmm", the headmaster pursed his lips. "Therein lies the problem." His tone was measured. "I have sympathy with you, I really do. But you see, we are in the minority. I fear it would damage the reputation of the school if it got out that we had a conscientious objector on staff. The governors would certainly protest as would the parents, fearing their boys were being indoctrinated with God knows what!" He attempted a laugh which turned into a clearing of the throat. "Anyway, I can't really take the risk. So, I've been speaking to a relative of mine who's a colonel in the army, explained our situation and he's come up with a solution that should keep everyone happy".

"Is he ending the war?" Jack asked.

The headmaster pursed his lips again. "I'm trying to help you, Foister. He suggested you apply for exemption because of poor eyesight. He said they could probably 'arrange' it easily enough for an exemption partly on grounds of physical fitness. That way, you don't have to compromise your beliefs and we don't have the problems of having a conchie on staff".

He sat back in his chair with a flourish, obviously waiting for Jack's grateful thanks. Jack looked down, pinching his nose as he took the suggestion on board. Ironically, his eyesight was so poor that he probably would be rejected anyway, but somehow, that wasn't the point. With a deep intake of breath, he looked up again.

"I appreciate the effort you've made. But my reason for not fighting is because I fundamentally believe that all warfare is wrong. If I request an exemption for any other reason, I would be compromising my beliefs and worse than that, I'd be a coward".

After this meeting with his headmaster, everything happened with frightening speed. Jack applied for total exemption from military service at the Peterborough local tribunal as he had intended. He made it clear that his objection wasn't made on Christian grounds, because his faith had been badly shaken by the Church's attitude to the war. Not unexpectedly, his application was turned down and Jack appealed.

Before the appeal hearing could be arranged, Jack was ordered to report for duty on 23 May. Because he had no intention of doing this, he knew he would face arrest. Although it was still only April, almost a month before he was due to report for duty, Jack didn't want to experience the humiliation of being arrested at school, so he took the decision to leave his teaching position and wait at home for events to take their course.

James Landers, 22, Bench Hand from Salford

In the summer of 1916, James Landers applied for absolute exemption from the provisions of the Military Service Act on two counts: first on grounds of conscience and second on the grounds that his mother would be left in dire hardship should he be forced to leave her. The local tribunal in Salford refused his application outright and he appealed to a regional tribunal. In preparation for his appeal, James gathered testimonials to support his claims, both to the poor health of his mother and to the sincerity of his religious faith.

Ironically, one of the people he turned to for help was the workmate with whom he had regular battles: Bill Hardy.

"You want me to what?" Bill said in disbelief.

"I just need you to write a letter saying how long you've known me, that I am a member of the Christian Brethren and my beliefs are sincere. You don't need to say that you support me, or even agree with me".

"Unbelievable!" Bill said, shaking his head. "What makes you think I'd help you?"

"Because you know why I object to the war and you know my beliefs are sincere. We've argued about it often enough".

"Why can't one of your Brethren pals write something for you? They'd be a damn sight more convincing than I would be".

"Because the tribunal wouldn't expect the Brethren to do anything *but* support me. They're less likely to believe a testimonial from them than from a colleague who doesn't even like me very much". Bill shook his head again and made to turn away, but James caught his arm.

"Bill, please? Apart from anything else, my mother is ill. Thrown in prison or killed by the Hun; either way, who's going to look after her when I'm not here?" The older man looked James in the eye, searching for the slightest hint of artifice and found nothing but clear, blue openness.

"I must be mad", he said and let out a long breath.

"You'll do it?"

"Yes I'll do it. But don't expect me to say anything about agreeing with you. Personally, I'd see all cowards lined up against the wall and shot". It was a bait, but James knew better than to take it. Instead he gave a rare smile and offered his hand to Bill who looked down at it before turning his back on James and walking away.

The regional tribunal rejected the claim that James's mother would be left in serious hardship but accepted, with the aid of Bill's testimony, that his religious faith was genuine. On 5 September 1916, James Landers was granted partial exemption from military service and ordered to join the Non-Combatant Corps. This presented him with a further dilemma; his first reaction was to stick to his principles and refuse to join the NCC, but turning to the Bible for guidance he was troubled by a particular verse in Timothy: 'But if any provide not for his own, and especially for those of his own house, he hath denied the faith and is worse than an infidel'. James knew that if he stuck to his absolutist principles, he would be imprisoned with no pay and would be unable to provide for his mother, so he accepted the ruling and prepared to join the NCC.

Charles Dingle, 18, Student from Southampton

Charles Dingle received his call up papers in the spring of 1916, while still at college. Determined to stand by his Christian pacifist beliefs despite the painful estrangement with his father, Charles applied for absolute exemption to military service on grounds of conscience. Like most men in his position, he found the tribunal largely unsympathetic but they ruled that, as Charles was still only 18 and needed the consent of his parents in order to serve overseas, he would be excused but was expected to 'come quietly' when he turned 19.

As the end of the college year approached, and with his birthday only a couple of months away, Charles gave a lot of thought to how he was going to handle the next tribunal. He wasn't averse to helping the war effort in some way, but couldn't see how to do this without becoming involved in the military machine and perpetuating the war. The answer came when his minister, the Reverend John Morris, introduced Charles to one of his friends, Liberal MP and Quaker, Edmund Harvey. Harvey, along with another Quaker MP, Arnold Rowntree, had been instrumental in drafting the part of the Military Service Act covering conscientious objection. Harvey introduced Charles to the secretary of the Friends Ambulance Unit (FAU) and Charles made the decision to join. He worried that perhaps he had taken the easy route; a couple of his friends had been given a rough ride at tribunals and made it clear that they thought he was using the FAU as an excuse to avoid standing up for his principles.

Having had no contact with his father since their confrontation in February, Charles decided to write and tell him of his plans to serve with the FAU. In part, Charles hoped his decision would appease his father, but it seemed to make things worse. The very terse reply he received was so formal that it could have been from a complete stranger and reiterated his father's view that unless Charles joined the RAMC at the very least, then he would have nothing more to do with him.

"I don't understand". Charles said to his mother after she'd read the letter. "I suppose I could understand if I wasn't prepared to do anything at all, but the Friends Ambulance Unit has a really important role to play. Can't he see that?"

"It's not the army though is it? By law you should be in the army like every other young man. It's the fact that you're *avoiding* military service that he finds so difficult to bear. Why won't you consider the RAMC? You would be doing the same kind of work as the Friends Ambulance Unit and it would resolve things with your father".

Charles sighed and sat down heavily in an armchair. There was so much sense in his mother's reasoning that it was hard to argue against.

"I'm not sure I can explain this very well. I certainly didn't manage it with dad", he began. "I can't reconcile my faith in God with the use of guns and explosives, I don't want to play any part in the killing of others. The RAMC is the military and supports the war. If I join them, I will be part of the military and so I'll also be supporting the war. Does that make any sense?"

He looked up at her, hoping for understanding. She blinked at him in silence for a moment before stepping across the room and pulling him gently to her.

"When did you become so grown up?" She sighed, kissing the top of his head. "It makes perfect sense and I'm proud of you for being so principled". She sat down in the chair next to him. "Your father is just going to have to get used to it and he will, sooner or later. In the meantime, we need to make plans".

Because the FAU was an entirely voluntary unit, expenses incurred in relation to uniform and training were met by the volunteers themselves. At 18, Charles could not cover these expenses himself and his father refused to help. Determined not to be beaten, Charles's mother wrote to the FAU explaining the situation and asking for financial assistance, which was duly granted. Charles attended the FAU training camp at Jordans in Buckinghamshire, before joining the hospital ship *Glenart Castle* as an orderly. While celebrating his nineteenth birthday on board, an officer with the RAMC warned Charles that he should be handed over to the authorities for not reporting for military service but added that as he was serving with the FAU, he would 'overlook it for now'.

David Blelloch, 21, Student at Oxford University

David Blelloch's call up papers instructed him to report to the recruiting office at 90 High Street, Oxford on 22 March 1916. Throughout his university career, David's socialist principles had matured and he planned to apply for absolute exemption from military service on grounds of conscience, though he saw his objection as purely political. As with most applications for exemption on conscientious grounds that were not religious, David was given short shrift by the tribunal and ordered to report for military service as instructed. With no intention of reporting, David continued with his everyday life and waited for his inevitable arrest.

Two police officers arrived at David's lodgings early one morning, with the intention of apprehending him before he left. Assuring them he would come quietly, the constables allowed David to finish shaving and dressing and spared him the humiliation of handcuffs. In fact, they rarely needed to use the handcuffs when it came to arresting 'conchies'. Fully prepared to dislike the 'slackers' and ready for a bit of a scuffle, the police had been surprised at how polite and co-operative the men were.

"Gentlemen most of 'em", one constable remarked to his friend in the pub one evening. "Not a bit like your regular criminals at all. Doesn't seem right, locking the likes of them in a cell".

But lock David in a cell they did, in the basement under Oxford police station. He found himself in the company of Victor Murray, a Methodist and fellow conscientious objector. Victor was much older than David; he was tall, balding and gaunt with a yellowish pallor. A persistent cough, which got progressively worse as the day wore on, made his imprisonment seem even more outrageous.

"How old are you? I mean, if you don't mind my asking?"

David said.

"Forty-one next month", Victor replied, smiling "and yes, I know I look much older".

"You're right at the limit of conscription age. Why on earth are they bothering to put you through all this?"

"I suppose the law is the law, even if I was a day away from 41". He shrugged before another fit of coughing left him weak and slumped on the bare boards that served as beds.

"There's no way you're fit enough for military service. Why didn't you just go along for your medical? You were bound to be declared unfit".

"I suppose I could have done, but then you see, it would have been taking the easy way out. It would have looked as though I was willing to fight and take part in the war, when I am most definitely not willing to do either".

David nodded, understanding. After another couple of coughing fits, David asked a constable to bring Victor a hot drink and, after taking one look at the older man slumped against the cell wall, the constable couldn't refuse.

"What the hell are we doing arresting sick old men anyway?" he grumbled to his sergeant as he waited for the kettle to boil.

"Less of the 'old' thank you", mumbled the 45-year-old sergeant into his newspaper.

After spending a night in the police cell, David and Victor were handed over to the military and given attestation forms to sign. Both refused to sign, despite considerable pressure from the recruiting officer, and spent the next night sleeping on boards in the guardroom of Cowley Barracks, before being presented to the medical officer for examination. Victor went before David and as he walked into the room, the medical officer did a double take. By now, Victor was drained of all colour apart from dark smudges beneath his eyes from lack of sleep.

"Have you spent the night in the guardroom?" the officer asked.

"I have. And the night before that in a police cell", Victor said affably.

"Good God!" the officer muttered, followed by something along the lines of the war robbing the world of its common sense. He ran through the protocol of examining Victor before declaring him totally unfit for service and released him immediately. When it was David's turn, the officer raised his eyebrows again.

"How old are you?" he asked, flicking through his notes.

"Twenty one". It was almost impossible not to say 'Sir', but David was determined not to show deference to army rank.

"There's not much of you for your age is there?" the officer said, regarding David's slight build. The officer examined him and, to David's surprise, placed him in a medical category so low that the military had no use for him and he too was released. It seemed that his health had still not fully recovered from the effects of the typhoid in 1913.

Now that David was under no obligation to serve with the military, he felt a compulsion to be of some use, as long as he wasn't actively contributing to the war. Although he wasn't a Quaker, David had several friends who were and he had nothing but admiration and respect for them as an organisation. The FAU provided him with the opportunity he needed to be useful.

Walter Roberts, 20, Architecture Student from Manchester

Walter Roberts first came to the attention of Fenner Brockway on the eve of his tribunal appearance in Stockport. Looking much younger than his 20 years, Walter was a quiet, yet charismatic man who seemed to capture the imagination and respect of anyone who met him. Having had a traditional Christian upbringing, Walter like so many other COs, found warfare incompatible with his religious faith. His father before him had taken a pacifist stance during the Boer War, so conscientious objection was a natural path for Walter. He joined the NCF in 1915 and actively campaigned against conscription in his local area.

Fenner Brockway described their first meeting and Walter's tribunal hearing in an article for *The Tribunal* in September 1916. Brockway was so impressed by Walter's quiet self-assurance and sincerity that he decided to cancel a prior engagement in order to be present at Walter's hearing, which also happened to be one of the earliest cases of a conscientious objector coming before a tribunal.

The tribunal comprised five local dignitaries, all experienced men as well as the requisite khaki-clad military representative.

It was his job to secure as many recruits as possible from these tribunal hearings and make sure no one got away lightly.

"I understand that you object to military service on the grounds that it is incompatible with your Christian principles", the chairman began.

"That is correct sir, yes", Walter's voice was crisp and clear.

"Aren't you a bit young to be holding such firm opinions?" a councillor asked him, peering over his glasses.

"I have been taught from my mother's knee that to hate and to kill is contrary to the teaching of Christ". Again, Walter's voice rang out with confident clarity. The members of the tribunal looked at one another; they were unused to being spoken to in such a manner by someone so young. They were torn between being impressed by his demeanour and irritated by his impudence.

A perfunctory interrogation began; Walter was asked whether he would be willing to undertake a non-combatant role; what sacrifices was he prepared to make for his country that would not violate his conscience and how did he reconcile his enjoyment of the privileges of British citizenship with his refusal to defend his country? Finally, the military representative asked him what he would do if attacked by a man with knife or sword. If there was a gun to hand, would he not defend himself with it? Walter met the man with a level gaze. "No Sir, I would not".

"What, if the man was intent on killing you, you would not use the gun to defend yourself?" the officer repeated in disbelief.

"No Sir, I would not. The sixth commandment states "Thou shalt not kill", so I would not kill him in order to save myself".

The hearing was brought to a close and four days later Walter heard that all exemption had been denied. He appealed and at the regional tribunal in Stockport his father spoke passionately in support of Walter's religious convictions, but it was to no avail and he was again refused all exemption. While awaiting his arrest, Walter continued supporting both the NCF and the Independent Labour Party, he attended rallies and handed out leaflets to anyone who would listen.

Brockway next encountered Walter Roberts on 16 May 1916 on a train journey from Manchester to London. The train had pulled

45

into Stockport station and Brockway could hear voices singing 'The Red Flag':

> *Then raise the scarlet standard high.*
> *Within its shade we'll live and die,*
> *Though cowards flinch and traitors sneer,*
> *We'll keep the red flag flying here.*

Cheers were raised on the platform and Brockway spotted a small group of absentees, including Walter, under military escort and being applauded by a group of ILP supporters. The group were led onto the train and found space in the same carriage as Brockway. Walter was in good spirits and seemed to be the one the others looked to for leadership, particularly a young lad who had been overwhelmed by the court process and was close to tears. In preparation for the journey, Walter had brought along a packed lunch which he shared, even giving a slice of his mother's homemade cake to one of the soldiers escorting them. By the time they left the train in Crewe, all the COs had made a positive impression on the other passengers.

"What a nice young chap he was", a businessman sitting opposite Brockway commented. "It's a shame that men who think it's wrong to fight should be treated this way". The businessman turned out to be a munitions manufacturer on his way to a meeting with Lloyd George and he was now determined to let the minister know how he felt about the situation if he had the chance.

For refusing to participate in any kind of work that would contribute to the war effort, Walter Roberts was imprisoned at the end of May 1916.

Jack Foister, James Landers, Charles Dingle, David Blelloch and Walter Roberts along with many thousands of others, were in the early stages of exercising what they believed to be their legal right to object to joining the army on conscientious grounds. They weren't slackers, or troublemakers; they were men from all classes and backgrounds, from factories, mills, universities, colleges and farms.

In the early stages of 1916, neither the men, the army nor the government fully understood the implications of the decisions being made. The conscience clause was designed to exempt men from taking up arms but it did not make provision for those who didn't want to support the war in any context whatsoever. For those men, the next few years would be a very bleak and uncertain time indeed, as first the army tried to break them while the government struggled to find a more humane way of handling them.

The stories within the following chapters are tales of intrigue and underhandedness; brutality; imprisonment; death-threats and enforced labour; as a country at war tried to deal with the men who dared to say no.

The Courage of Cowards

CHAPTER 4

THE FRIENDS AMBULANCE UNIT

To care for him who shall have borne the battle...
(Abraham Lincoln, Second Inaugural Address, 1865)

The Friends Ambulance Unit (FAU) began in the autumn of 1914 as a group of 43 men, supported by a donation of £100. By the end of the war there were 600 men in France and Flanders alone and throughout the course of the war the unit had received a total of £138,000 in voluntary contributions. The 43 men who left London for Belgium in September 1914 did so with the best of intentions, but with no real idea of whether they could be useful. By November 1918, the FAU had become responsible for a whole network of ambulance and hospital services, including ambulance trains and hospital ships. Between 1915 and 1918, the FAU established hospitals at Dunkirk, Ypres, Poperinghe and Hazebrouck, as well as at York, Birmingham, London and Richmond.

The foundation of an entirely voluntary ambulance service is a remarkable feat and one that bears some explanation. Members of the Society of Friends, or Quakers, opposed anything that may harm their fellow man and would play no part in the fighting of a war. However, core to Quaker principles are the concepts of equality and fellowship, so many were not content to simply stand aside while the conflict raged around them. Appalled by the news from Belgium of casualties and dispossessed civilians, the Quaker Philip Baker, a talented academic and athlete who had competed for Britain in the 1912 Olympic Games, formed a group

49

whose intention was to help the relief effort and provide some form of medical aid.

After replying to an appeal for volunteers in the *Friend* on 21 August, a group of around 60 young Friends attended a newly established training camp at the village of Jordans in Buckinghamshire. At this stage no one knew when, or even if, the men may be called upon; whether they would be permitted overseas or what kind of service they would be allowed to provide, so the training aimed to cover every eventuality: first aid; sanitation and hygiene; field cookery and physical training. After six weeks of negotiating with the military, it looked as though there would be no practical use for the small, voluntary unit and the training camp was closed down.

At the end of October though, the Belgian Army suffered enormous losses at Yser as they strove to defend the Channel ports, and their medical resources were unable to cope. Philip Baker knew the Friends Ambulance Unit had a role to play and approached the Chairman of the Joint War Committee, the Hon Arthur Stanley MP, who agreed to allow the newly-designated First Anglo-Belgian Ambulance Unit into Belgium as a matter of urgency.

On the last day of October 1914, 43 men including three doctors and six dressers, set sail from Dover with eight ambulance cars. A few miles into the Channel, they came across the cruiser *Hermes*; she had been torpedoed and was sinking rapidly. The crew and Friends volunteers became involved in a hasty, unexpected rescue operation before turning back to Dover with the dead and injured. They finally sailed into Dunkirk as the sun set that evening; the sea was calm and there was little to mark their arrival in a war zone apart from the occasional, distant roar of a heavy gun.

The men were preparing to spend the night on board ship when they received news that was to give them a shocking introduction to the effects of warfare. Thousands of wounded French soldiers were pouring into the evacuation sheds at Dunkirk railway station. The authorities were overwhelmed and unable to cope with the numbers, having only six men to attend to the 3,000 currently lying in the goods sheds.

When the raw, inexperienced Friends volunteers arrived at

the sheds they were confronted with a charnel scene. Hundreds upon hundreds of men lay on straw covered floors, many had been there for several days, untended and unfed; the dead and the dying side by side. Most of those still living were exhausted, in extreme pain and despair; the stench of death and gangrene was overpowering. The young Friends who worked in the sheds that night would never forget the horror of it. But one thing was certain: there was an indisputable need for the First Anglo-Belgian Ambulance Unit to provide emergency medical support. Throughout the months that followed, the unit grew in both size and reputation, although its operations were still somewhat unco-ordinated. For instance, there was no established network and ambulance units travelled ad hoc to wherever they were needed. By the summer of 1915 though, the unit, now dubbed the 'Friends Ambulance Unit', had developed an organised structure able to respond quickly and efficiently to the needs of the war.

One of the biggest problems facing the FAU was manpower; it relied entirely upon unpaid volunteers and as the size and shape of the unit changed, it variously had too many volunteers or too few. In the early months, volunteers came and went as their circumstances changed and it was impossible to maintain an efficient service on these terms. With the introduction of conscription in January 1916 and the allowance for conscientious objection, there was an increased flow of volunteers for the FAU as an alternative to military service. This allowed the FAU to formalise a structure whereby volunteers had to commit to serving for a full six months, followed by subsequent periods of three months. A stable number of men allowed the unit to take on more permanent work without the fear of not having enough men to fulfil its obligations.

With the increasingly steady flow of volunteers that resulted from conscription, however, came the risk that the FAU may be inundated with men using the unit as a way of avoiding military service; men who would never have volunteered otherwise. As a consequence, the unit was careful to ensure that it only recruited those men referred to it by the tribunals or military authorities and that those referrals were already members of the Society of Friends.

When it was at its strongest, the FAU provided not only medical services, but also approved 'national work' in England, in agriculture or education, for example. A man volunteering for the FAU could choose to serve in a hospital in England or Belgium, an ambulance in France or Belgium, a hospital ship, offices, farms – the list goes on. A volunteer could do anything from admin work to cleaning out slops, or rescuing wounded men under bombardment.

Whatever their role, these men found a way of providing help and support for those affected by war without compromising their beliefs. The two accounts that follow reveal what life was like for men who chose the Friends Ambulance Unit.

David Blelloch

Having been exempted from military service on medical grounds, David Blelloch was willing to undertake some kind of 'war work' as long as it didn't contribute to the continuance of the war. Although not a Quaker himself, David had several friends who were and he respected the Quakers as an organisation. He was recommended to the Friends Ambulance Unit by one of those friends, who offered David the ideal opportunity to 'do his bit'. In June 1916 he became a ward orderly in a military hospital. Falling quickly into the mundane but arduous hospital routines of scrubbing floors, serving meals, washing up and collecting bedpans, David was content that he had found the right balance for his conscience.

After two months David was assigned to the hospital ship the *Glenart Castle*, and set sail for Salonika (now *Thessalonika*) in Greece. The *Glenart Castle* was an impressive, modern and well-equipped floating hospital, with beds for 460 patients and accommodation for five doctors, 12 sisters and nurses, 40 orderlies, as well as 111 ordinary crew. Each ward had electric lights, copper percolators, sterilizers, wash basins, tables etc and in addition to the wards there was a disinfecting room, X-ray room, operating theatre, soda water house and laundry. There were even hand-operated lifts for lowering patients on stretchers from the deck to the wards.

Dealing largely with cases of malaria, the *Glenart Castle* made several trips between Salonika and Malta and sometimes transported patients from the Greek Islands to the giant cruise liner the *Britannic*, also fitted out as a hospital ship. When the *Britannic* took a direct hit on the morning of 21 November 1916 it sank in under an hour although, unlike her infamous sister ship the *Titanic*, well over a thousand people escaped with their lives and less than 30 perished.

On the whole, David's life aboard the *Glenart Castle* seemed to pass with relatively few crises, until she was torpedoed by a U-boat during her return to England in March 1917. Fortunately, on this occasion she was only damaged and, although listing badly, she did not sink and all on board escaped alive. David was involved in the evacuation of the ship, helping patients up onto the deck to await rescue. Once those patients able to walk had been organised, the orderlies began to evacuate those less able. David ran to a bed at the far end of a ward and slid to a halt. Slightly built and nudging 5ft 6in, David gawped at the patient in the bed with his leg strapped up, he was broad, heavy and at least 6ft tall.

"Are you it, then?" the patient asked nervously.

"Afraid so", David said apologetically, after scanning the ward for alternatives.

"How on earth are you going to manage to get me up two decks?"

"I'm stronger than I look", David offered.

"Are you taller than you look too?"

"Look, you've only got one leg out of action haven't you... Phillips?" David said, squinting at the chart hooked over the end of the bed. "Let's give it a go rather than stand here debating my shortcomings, shall we? Before we actually sink".

With considerable effort, David managed to heave Phillips out of bed and with one arm firmly around his shoulders, they managed to hobble across the now sloping floor of the ward towards the only available exit. Phillips cursed under his breath at the pain of dragging his leg awkwardly behind him. They reached the exit and stopped; they were facing a steep, narrow stairway, little better than a ladder. They looked at one another and David shrugged. "I'll have to carry you", he said and Phillips snorted.

"I'd laugh if I wasn't in so much pain", he said.

"Any other ideas?" David asked, starting to feel irritated. Hunching over, David stood in front of Phillips and took both the man's arms over his shoulders. "Lock your arms together", he said, "and try not to choke me". With a deep breath, he grasped the hand-rails of the stairway and began to climb, taking Phillips's considerable weight on his shoulders. He reached the top just as he felt his legs buckle with the effort; pulling himself up straight, he dropped Phillips awkwardly onto his good leg.

"I'll be damned!" Phillips said appreciatively. "Wouldn't have put money on that, not in a million years".

"We've another one to do yet". David said, with an increasing sense of urgency and wondering if he could manage the same feat twice. The *Glenart Castle* was listing noticeably now and the orderliness of the evacuation was beginning to falter. The two men staggered with the crowds towards the next exit, where David hauled Phillips onto his shoulders once more; it was a real struggle this time, with David's legs shaking violently under the strain.

Someone coming up the ladders behind them shouted: "It's alright mate, I've got him".

And David felt the burden on his shoulders ease as Phillips's weight was partly supported from below. When they reached the top, David fell to his knees and Phillips slid heavily off his back, howling with pain.

"Sorry!" David said, scrambling to help Phillips up.

"No need to apologise", Phillips grinned despite the pain. "I reckon I deserved that for being so rude to you. Regular little Hercules you are".

David didn't return to the *Glenart Castle* after this episode; a decision that possibly saved his life, because the unarmed, clearly marked hospital ship was torpedoed by another U-boat on 26 February 1918. This time she wasn't so lucky; the torpedo strike was catastrophic and she sank in under ten minutes, so quickly in fact that there wasn't enough time to launch all the lifeboats. In total, 162 people were killed, including the captain, eight nurses, seven medical officers of the RAMC and 47 orderlies, some of whom would have been with the FAU and conscientious objectors.

Instead, David spent the remainder of the war at FAU Headquarters in Malo-les-Bains, near Dunkirk, engaged in the mundanity of kitchen work, filling sandbags and loading truckloads of granite setts.

Charles Dingle

Charles Dingle was on board the *Glenart Castle* at the same time as David Blelloch, although it's not clear from either man's records whether or not they knew one another or even met. Charles's experiences on board the *Glenart Castle* were similar to David's and he too left the ship after she was torpedoed in March 1917.

For his next assignment, Charles chose to serve on board an Ambulance Train (AT) carrying wounded soldiers from the Western Front, a choice that would take this quiet, unassuming conscientious objector right into the heart of some of the most ferocious fighting of the war. On 19 August, 1917 Charles Dingle joined AT No 17 and his diary records the details of the train with evident pride. AT17 had 16 Great Eastern coaches; five of these were 'cot' wards fitted out with bunks for the severely wounded; five were 'sitting' wards for the less severely wounded and five were service coaches. She could take 500 patients and was staffed by three doctors, three nurses and 47 orderlies.

It is hard to imagine how three doctors and three nurses could possibly manage up to 500 wounded men in such cramped and challenging conditions, but the railway was without doubt the fastest, most efficient way of removing patients from the often insanitary and perilous conditions of the casualty clearing stations near the Front.

On the whole, Charles's diary for this period records only minor details of his daily routine, but enough to give a clear picture of what life on board AT17 was like. He quickly settled into a pattern of life that juxtaposed periods of frenzied activity – carrying wounded men onto the train, installing them into carriages, dressing wounds and changing bandages – with long periods of quiet boredom as the train waited in sidings. Living in constant close proximity with the other orderlies, Charles began to build firm friendships with men who held similar Christian pacifist views to his own.

One particular event, however, had such an impact on Charles's life that he chose to write a separate account additional to his diary; an account that makes for extraordinary reading. It is the evening of 20 March 1918 and Charles begins his account thus: 'The evening was warm and enchanting, all around was quiet and peaceful', which seems the most unlikely of beginnings for an account of war, but Charles makes a habit of recording beauty wherever he finds it throughout his diaries, perhaps as a way of clinging on to some notion of sanity in the world.

AT17 is in sidings at La Chapellette in Peronne, on the banks of the Somme, and Charles is out walking with his friend W. Farley Rutter, referred to only as 'Rutter'. Charles and Rutter stand on the banks of a canal, watching the sun setting over the war-stricken country, the deep golden light making the 'solemn scene less depressing than usual'. They reminisce about home and wonder how long it will be before they see their families again. Charles remembers the tranquility of this evening with such clarity because of the carnage that was to follow. The men were aware that the Germans were preparing for a 'push' and, while they knew that the crew of AT17 would be up for a difficult time, they didn't realise just how sudden and how devastating the advance would be.

On the morning of 21 March, AT17 leaves Peronne to travel the seven miles to the town of Tincourt. As they travel they hear the sound of tremendous bombardment in the distance; the noise increases steadily as they approach Tincourt until eventually shells are bursting all around the train and shrapnel is falling close by. Charles and his fellow orderlies are tasked with evacuating Casualty Clearing Station No 5 at Tincourt, which is caught up in the bombardment and needs to be moved from danger. It is a hurried operation, the walking wounded are helped, chivvied and pushed along; the more seriously wounded are carried onto the train by any means possible. The noise is intense and the bombardment terrifyingly close; one wayward shell could spell disaster. Eventually, the train is loaded and heads west, away from danger, arriving in Rouen at midnight.

The next morning, AT17 heads back to the front lines and the small town of Ham. Before reaching Ham, the train pulls up at the nearby town of Nesle. Told to stay on the train and await further instruction, Charles pushes open a window and leans out to view a scene of utter chaos. Nesle station is packed with crowds of civilians evacuated from the districts of Ham and Nesle; mothers clinging onto babies, small children and the elderly all clutching scanty, hastily-packed baggage. There is an air of controlled fear, punctuated by the sound of crying babies and the shouts of mothers trying to locate children lost in the crowd. Charles is used to dealing with frightened, wounded soldiers, but this is something altogether different.

"What are you looking at?" Rutter said, clapping Charles on the back and making him jump.

"All these poor souls", Charles says, leaning to one side so Rutter can see over his shoulder. "Really brings it home to you doesn't it? They're just ordinary people and they've lost everything. Can you imagine if this was home? They could be our families and loved ones". The two men look on in silence as officials make feeble attempts to induce some order to the crowd and bewildered people try to shuffle to the most favourable positions for the arrival of the next train.

The sound of gunfire overhead suddenly grabs everyone's attention; both Charles and Rutter lean further out of the window and strain to look up. British and German planes are wheeling around over the town, two of them engaged in a dog fight. The British plane is chasing the German, firing short bursts of fury. They disappear over the top of the train and out of Charles and Rutter's view.

"Get out of the train!" Rutter yells.

"We're not supposed to..." Charles begins, but Rutter pushes him out of the way, reaches down and opens the door. Both men jump down onto the track and look up, shielding their eyes against the sun. They watch as the planes swoop and turn; the British plane fires again, this time finding its target and a streak of black smoke pours from the German plane's engine before the whole machine bursts into flames. Rutter lets out a yelp and Charles puts his hands to his face as they watch two figures leap from the plane and fall towards the ground, landing out of view behind a building.

"Get back on the train!" is barked at them from a nearby open door and they clamber back on board, shocked and, although reluctant to admit it, exhilarated by what they have witnessed.

AT17 remains at Nesle awaiting instruction to proceed to Ham. To pass the time, Charles and Rutter play Bezique, a game that Rutter has a flair for and Charles is constantly striving to improve on. Another orderly by the name of Quinn leans in the doorway, a short young man with tortoiseshell glasses and pale brown hair so fine it looks like it is thinning already. He digs out a packet of cigarettes.

"Have you heard the latest?" Quinn asks.

"About what?" Charles is frowning over his cards.

"Ham. Looks like we won't be going after all", Quinn says, lighting a cigarette and drawing deeply on it. Both Charles and Rutter look up from their cards. Quinn, having shaken out his match, flicks it expertly through the nearest open window.

"The track's been blown out for a start, so it's doubtful we'd get through. Apparently it's carnage out there, Ham's being shelled and they're evacuating the CCS by motor vehicle".

"They'll never get everyone out without a train". Rutter says.

"Oh they've got a train". Quinn added. "AT6 is out there. Problem is, it can't get back".

The three men look at one another, all thinking the same thing: that could have been us.

Luckily, AT6 did manage to get back later that evening; its windows smashed from shellfire en route. About an hour later, the crew of AT17 are told they are heading in the opposite direction towards Marchelepot. Charles still hasn't decided whether he is relieved about this decision or not when Rutter, who is peering through the window, says something disturbing:

"We're going the wrong way".

"What?" Charles exclaims, almost laughing.

"We are you know! We're heading towards Ham!" Charles jumps up to join him at the window, frantically peering for landmarks.

"Look, see that rise in the ground over there, with the trees? And the big barn to the right?" Rutter points out. "We're going to Ham".

He is right, they both knew the area well and there is no denying it. Word spreads up and down the train, but no one seems to know why they are heading in the wrong direction. There is nothing to do but sit and wait for instruction.

As they travel, the countryside around them changes; fresh craters pit the earth, woodland relatively intact the last time AT17 passed this way is now broken, shattered trees expose bare wood, ragged trunks are snapped in two. Smoke hangs in the air, a menacing fog erasing the distant horizon; the flames of a recently shelled farmhouse, blazing. Shells fall around the tracks throwing earth up against the windows and making the coaches rock. The men sit in silence now, their conversation and humour abated.

Suddenly, the train jerks violently; the men grab the nearest fixed object to prevent being thrown over. With a deafening squeal, judder and hiss of steam, the train is brought to a halt so abruptly that Charles and his friends can't prevent themselves from falling; books, playing cards, pens, bags, boxes – anything that isn't fixed flies along the coach. When the chaos comes to an end the men pick themselves up, rubbing their shoulders, elbows and knees slammed down.

"Well, we're still upright, so I suppose that's a good thing", Charles says, tipping his head back and wincing, he rubs his neck just as a shell explodes close enough to the track to fling earth and shrapnel over the train. The men instinctively duck.

"Do you think we've been hit?" Rutter says.

"Maybe, though we'd have heard more of an explosion surely?" Quinn asks, squinting at the twisted arm of his spectacles.

Charles and Rutter go to the end of the coach, push the window down and tentatively lean out. The train is intact, no holes appear to have been blown in her sides; another two shells explode, one after another but far enough away this time not to threaten AT17. At the front of the train, they can see the engine driver jump down off the footplate; a small group of uniforms have gathered around what turns out to be the Ham chief of police, who is shouting and gesticulating wildly at them. Another shell screams over and explodes close enough to make the group of uniforms dive to the ground before clambering back on board, leaving the Ham chief of police to run back towards his car.

Word travels down the coaches that if AT17 had carried on any further, they would have run out of track and passed onto bare earth. The situation at Ham is so dire that the British have retreated and blown up the station and tracks in preparation for the arrival of the Germans. The engine begins to doggedly push AT17 back up the tracks in the direction of Nesle. A shell explodes on the line directly behind the engine, opening up a crater and destroying the track completely.

"That was a bit close for comfort", Quinn says, still trying to set right the arm of his spectacles.

"Too close", Charles answers. "The engine is travelling backwards, but the Hun doesn't know that. They aimed directly at us. If we'd still been travelling forwards, that shell would have hit the train and we'd all be dead".

It was a sobering thought and one that kept the men quiet for some time.

The journey of AT17 back towards Nesle then on to its original destination of Marchelepot is a difficult and traumatic one. Every CCS it calls at along the way is in a state of panic, men with every conceivable injury are loaded onto the train. Some CCSs have to evacuate so quickly that it's impossible to remove all the patients and so volunteers stay behind to care for them and await capture when the Germans arrive, which they do within a matter of days.

AT17 arrives in Marchelepot in the early hours of 23 March, offloads all the patients and heads straight back to the Front. There is a delay of nine hours because of an accident on the line and the men take the opportunity to catch up on much needed sleep, aware that what faces them may be even worse than the previous day.

Eventually, they arrive at the CCS at Dernancourt, nicknamed 'Edgehill' by British troops because of the rising ground to the north-west, to be confronted with chaos on a scale far beyond anything they had experienced before. There are several hundred walking wounded gathered in front of the CCS; filthy, exhausted, bandaged and in pain, many of them having walked the long miles from the front lines. The road is thronging with vehicles and troops; reinforcements heading out towards the Front and motor ambulances attempting to get to the CCS at Doullens, which is about to evacuate and unable to take further casualties. As well as AT17, there are two other ambulance trains and ordinary troop trains trying to accommodate the wounded and even then it seems doubtful that they will get everyone on board.

Charles and his fellow orderlies get to work loading as many men as the train can possibly handle. It is the worst loading they have ever encountered, moving casualties whose injuries are so extreme that by rights they should have been left to die in peace. There are men with limbs missing who haven't had any attention at the CCS; wounds not yet dressed; bodies shot to pieces. Charles thought he was used to seeing wounded men, anaesthetised to their plight and their fear, but this was far worse than he could have imagined.

"He's no more than a boy", Rutter says as they lift a stretcher bearing a young soldier missing his left arm and half of his face.

"Those bloody generals running this war should do some Red Cross work, we'll see how quick they change their views then", Charles replies with an uncharacteristic flash of anger.

Finally loaded up, AT17 begins its journey back towards Marchelepot. The German advance is so rapid now that the train travels through pockets of fighting and is fired upon; for a time, the crew fear that the train may actually fall into enemy hands. To make matters worse, the line through Amiens has been bombed and there is tremendous congestion on the remaining rail network, meaning that they can only crawl along, averaging about 600 yards an hour.

Travelling slowly through the night, under continuous bombardment, the wounded men need constant attention; some more than Charles or his colleagues can give. Through the course of the night, 10 men die and the combined stench of gangrenous wounds and corpses renders the atmosphere foul and nauseating.

One man, whose name Charles doesn't know and whose face is hidden behind dressings, had been close to an exploding shell and is riddled from head to feet with wounds. There is no chance of his survival. Swathed in bandages, he lies on a stretcher as there is no free bed; remaining conscious when unconsciousness would have been a blessing. He tosses and turns, writhes in pain, crying out for help and for his mother. There is nothing Charles can do to help him because he is beyond help, so Charles sits with him as much as he can through his long, tortuous final hours. He holds the man's hand and tries to soothe him, to calm him down. On 25 March, Charles makes a single entry in his diary: 'man died in my arms at 5am'.

AT17 eventually passes through Amiens on the morning of 26 March. There are now 23 corpses on board; the final leg of the journey to Rouen takes another six hours, during which time two more men die. When the train is offloaded in Rouen, Charles fights back tears as he realises the awful experience is finally over. It is 90 miles from Edgehill to Rouen and the journey has taken 50 hours, with an average of one death every two hours.

Charles remained with AT17 until the crew were disbanded on 2 February 1919. After the Armistice of 11 November 1918, the ambulance trains began clearing out the remaining casualties from areas of France and Belgium formerly occupied by the German Army. It was a steady, ordered and well-organised operation. The crews were no longer in imminent danger and could take the necessary time and care of the men they were rescuing; it was a slow relaxing of tension before being allowed to return home.

In all, AT17 made 375 trips between December 1915 and January 1919 and moved a total of 129,517 patients.

The stories of David Blelloch and Charles Dingle are quite different, but both are representative of the men who chose to serve with the Friends Ambulance Unit. These men weren't answering any call to arms, they weren't caught up in a sense of duty or nationalistic fervour; the men who joined the FAU did so because it was a voluntary, non-military organisation and had the principle of peace at its core.

David, despite objecting to military service on grounds of conscience, was actually exempted on medical grounds, so he could have easily remained in civilian life without anyone trying to heap a sense of shame on to him. Instead, he chose to help in a practical way, providing support for those caring for the wounded. Charles, on the other hand, joined the FAU in an attempt to balance his own pacifist views with the militarist views of his father. It was a compromise he was happy with and one that eventually appeased his father.

Whether it was the mundanity of cleaning bed pans and scrubbing floors or the horror of rescuing wounded men while under bombardment, every member of the FAU made a real difference to the lives of the men they cared for, even if only making their last few hours more bearable. Men who joined the FAU as an alternative to military service had reached a difficult and considered decision which would undoubtedly change them forever. This was no easy option to avoid 'facing the music', as many thought, including Charles Dingle's own father. Although they refused to take a life or to harm their fellow men, their lives too were often in danger; they too lost friends and peers; they too saw men die.

THE COURAGE OF COWARDS

CHAPTER 5

THE NON-COMBATANT CORPS
& WORK SCHEMES

Punished and Persecuted
(Ernest E. Hunter, *The Home Office Compounds: A Statement as to How Conscientious Objectors are Penalised,* **1917)**

Local tribunals granted very few men absolute exemption from military service on conscientious grounds and most were initially denied any form of exemption. After failing at their first tribunal, many went on to appeal and, if they could prove the sincerity of their objection, were usually granted a partial exemption. This exempted them from combatant service only and they were still expected to serve their country by joining either the Royal Army Medical Corps or the newly-formed Non-Combatant Corps, though the Friends Ambulance Unit was also seen as acceptable alternative service for Quakers.

At this point, conscientious objectors ceased to be an homogeneous group and were instead split into those who were not willing to support the war in any capacity – the absolutists – and those who were willing to support the war, as long as they did not have to take a life – the alternativists. If a man took the absolutist stance then he would very quickly find himself under arrest and facing a difficult and uncertain path through the war. If a man took the alternativist stance, his way forward was much clearer; he would join a military support unit of some kind and, if he co-operated, the war would pass by relatively smoothly.

The Non-Combatant Corps (NCC) was formed in March 1916 to coincide with the implementation of the Military Service Act. The government had been impressed with the organisation of the Friends Ambulance Unit (FAU) and were convinced that they could create a 'military' unit similar in structure to the FAU, which would provide valuable support for the army and also overcome conscientious objections to military service. The original plan for the NCC was for the unit to take part in transport duties, construction work and to facilitate supply. Not only was this work vital to the functioning of the army, it also freed up thousands of men who were willing to fight. The No Conscription Fellowship (NCF), representing the rights of conscientious objectors, vehemently opposed the NCC and advised their members to have no part in it because, in the words of Fenner Brockway, 'it assists in the taking of life and the prosecution of war'.

Those men who did accept the NCC as an alternative to combatant service soon realised that they were, to all intents and purposes, soldiers without guns; they were expected to wear khaki and to follow military orders. Often mocked and derided by the regular soldiers they worked alongside, the COs who joined the NCC appeared to both the general public and to the NCF to be taking the easy route: refusing to fight but not sticking entirely to their pacifist principles either.

James Landers

With his request for absolute exemption from military service denied, James Landers had compromised his beliefs and agreed to join the Non-Combatant Corps to provide financial support for his mother. James's first posting was to Kinmel Park, near the village of Bodelwyddan in North Wales, and as someone who naturally followed rules, he settled in well to his new routine.

Surrounded by other conscientious objectors holding broadly similar views on the war, James found he had more friends than in his former civilian life and he fell in with a group of Plymouth Brethren, an evangelical movement with the same roots as the Christian Brethren. Together the group took a room over the old smithy in Bodelwyddan, so that they could 'remember the Lord in the breaking of bread'. James was put in charge on the walk down to the village, because he could be trusted to ensure the other men saluted any officers they might encounter on the way.

It would appear that life for COs sent to Kinmel Park was not as arduous as at other similar army camps. As long as the COs towed the line and behaved themselves, they were treated with respect and granted certain freedoms. Even if they remained true to their absolutist principles and refused to obey orders, they were still treated with understanding. On 22 June 1916, some 50 COs detained in guard rooms at Kinmel Park awaiting court martial for disobeying orders, presented their guards with the most extraordinary gift imaginable under the circumstances: an autograph album.

The first page of the album is inscribed thus:

To whom it may concern

This book contains the signatures etc of many conscientious objectors who were detained in Guard Rooms 5 & 10, 19 camp, Kinmel Park.

They herein attempt to show their appreciation of the noble services rendered by Comrades Carter & Jones in bettering their position whilst confined in the Guard Rooms awaiting Court Martial for disobeying Military orders on conscientious grounds "<u>or words to that effect</u>".

The phrase 'or words to that effect' must have appeared so many times in the charge sheets of conscientious objectors everywhere that it was repeatedly satirised by the COs. The autograph album is filled with handwritten poems and ditties by the incarcerated men; some educated and well-written, others short and simple, but all showing gratitude to Carter and Jones for their treatment of the men. William Rees, wrote:

Little thought I when at Cardiff
Beaten in a cell so dark
That such friends as Jones and Carter
I should meet at Kinmel Park.

And another, W. Pugh: 'It is in times of disappointment and suffering that character is built up and stability gained. Socialism does not come by shouting –'.

Whether Carter and Jones sympathised with the conscientious objectors, or simply felt it right to treat their fellow men with compassion we can only guess, but they must have been immensely touched by such a show of appreciation.

If James could have spent the duration of the war at Kinmel Park, then he would probably have been perfectly happy, but the authorities had other ideas. The group of Plymouth Brethren were moved from Kinmel and posted instead to Latham Park in Ormskirk, where they were separated into different huts. James could see no reason for this other than the authorities' desire to break morale. The Army Service Corps was based at Latham Park and James was tasked with leading horses and mules from the train to the camp. Having no experience with either horses or mules, James found the task daunting, particularly when a mule unexpectedly kicked out its hind legs and split open the jaw of the man next to him.

When James was put on guard duty for the first time, Sergeant Robinson explained what was expected of him:

"And if you are approached by anyone, anyone at all mind, you should ask: '*Halt, who goes there, friend or foe?*' Alright?"

James shook his head, "No, I don't think I can say that". The sergeant stared at him blankly for a moment or two, not comprehending.

"What do you mean *you can't say that?*"

"Because, when the Lord knew him that came to Him to betray Him, he said 'Friend, whom seek ye?' so that is what I shall say if I am approached".

"Will you now?" the sergeant replied, narrowing his eyes and wondering whether this CO was taking the piss. James's face was impassive and the sergeant realised that the upstart was being serious.

"I'd rather you said what I've just told you to say", he growled menacingly. James stared dutifully ahead and made no reply, because he had no intention of following the sergeant's instruction.

Later that evening, James sat in the canteen nursing a mug of tea after his meal, when he heard what sounded like an argument somewhere behind him.

"Looks like trouble", said a friend next to him, nodding his head sideways. Turning round, James saw a regular soldier standing by a nearby table berating a fellow NCC.

"Enjoying your easy life are you? Sleep soundly at night, eh? Knowing there's no danger of a bullet coming your way? You're not fit to wear khaki at all, playing at being a soldier but never having to fight". He pushed the NCC man roughly. "Nothing but a coward, you should be ashamed".

James set his mug down and stood up. The soldier, tall and powerfully built, was leaning over the NCC man, who was still seated at the table trying to avoid giving him any provocation. James went and stood behind the soldier. He waited, arms crossed, for the man to stop talking, then tapped the soldier's arm.

"If you've quite finished, I'd like a few words please", he said calmly, oblivious to the soldier's raised eyebrow and clenched fist.

"I don't know what a conchie'd have to say that'd be of any interest to me".

"Sir, are you a Christian?" James asked

"Of course", the soldier answered.

"Then you will know that we are all accountable to God. You will know that God is all wise, all powerful and all love. If you accept that, then you must also accept how right and profitable it is to obey His commandments which so clearly state 'Thou Shalt Not Kill'. It is self-will and disobedience of God that has led to all sorrows; pain; corruption; man's injustice to man, to individuals, groups, cities, countries and empires".

The soldier un-clenched his fist and bit his lip. He had wanted an argument, a bit of a fight even; what he hadn't expected was this calm, self-possessed preaching. It was hard to want to punch someone so placid, where was the sport in that?

"God is ever seeking for those who would seek Him", James continued. Unaware of the soldier's changing countenance or of the gathering crowd of regulars behind him, he talked of loving thy neighbour and loving thine enemy and of the Lord 'sending His Son to be a Saviour'. Some of his fellow NCCs pushed to the front of the crowd, fearing James was about to be thumped.

When he finally stopped talking and realised how many men were glaring at him, it shook his composure for perhaps the first time. An NCC man took his arm and led him quickly through the nearest door, half-expecting to be followed and set upon. No one came after them; all the men remained behind in the canteen and began talking to one another, regulars and NCCs alike. Uncomfortable at first, some men made fun of James's preaching, but gradually they admitted respect for his courage in speaking up and avoiding a fight. The NCCs and the regulars had more time for one another after that evening, although James found it hard to take any credit for it.

At the beginning of 1918, the law changed to allow relatives of soldiers under punishment to continue receiving the pay allotted to them. For James Landers this meant that if he chose to stick to his principles absolutely and refuse to obey orders, then he would still be able to provide financial support for his mother. The decision was simple, the next time Sergeant Robinson ordered James to the stables, James refused to move, stating:

"According to my religious convictions, I shall have to disobey all military orders".

The sergeant's face fell; he'd been expecting this from half the NCCs under him. "Aw, come on lad! Don't do this!" he said. "You're a good lad at heart, a bit odd maybe, but there's no harm in you. You know they'll throw you in prison don't you? They're not all friendly conchies in there you know, there's some real bad buggers. Rapists and murderers. Do you really want to spend the rest of the war preaching to the likes of them? They'll eat you for breakfast".

James was intractable and was court martialled on 23 February 1918. Found guilty of refusing to obey an order, he was sent to Wormwood Scrubs.

For the first month in prison, James was kept in solitary confinement, as was common practice for COs; cells were typically 10ft long by 4ft wide and furnished with only a narrow bed and a night stand. The only time he was allowed out of his cell was for daily exercise, which involved parading around the prison yard in a circle, one man behind another exactly 8 yards apart, swinging their arms and forbidden from speaking to one another. Failure to comply with the rules resulted in bread and water rations.

After that first month, James was put into a work gang and passed his days breaking rocks and wheeling barrows; it was arduous and exhausting, but James bore it stoically because he knew his conscience was clear. One day he heard two prison officers discussing a problem with the governor's telephone and, being James, he didn't think twice about speaking up and offering to help.

"Before the war, I had a job at the telephone works up in Salford", he began when given permission to speak. "It's probably something quite simple. I'd be happy to have a look at it for you".

The officers looked at one another and shrugged. "I suppose it wouldn't do any harm to keep the governor happy".

Under the watchful eye of the officers, James was permitted the use of a tool kit, though they didn't stretch as far as offering him a chair. Kneeling down in front of the governor's desk, James dismantled the body of the telephone and smiled.

"It's just a loose wire, that's all. Thought it'd be something simple, there's not much can go wrong with these things".

Within a couple of minutes, he was putting the telephone back together.

"Would you care to try it out, Sir?" he said, standing up. The governor lifted the ear-piece and tapped the receiver, spoke briefly to the operator and replaced the ear-piece.

"Well done Landers, it's appreciated".

The following day, James found himself back in the governor's office, standing to attention and wondering what he'd done wrong.

"You're a conscientious objector, I see". The governor, a tall, wiry man with thin sandy hair and a neat moustache, looked James up and down, trying to determine whether he was a troublemaker or not.

"Yes sir".

"What are the grounds of your objection? Religious or political?"

"Religious sir".

"Hmmm", the governor nodded. "I can have an iota of sympathy with that I suppose. It's turned out to be a damned horrific business in the end, this war". He went back to his chair and sat down. "You strike me as a trustworthy sort of chap Landers. We

71

could do with someone on hand, so to speak, to do odd-jobs about the prison. Maintain the electric and gas lights and the bells and so on. Think you'd be up to that?"

James raised his eyebrows in surprise. "Yes sir".

"Good", the governor nodded again. "Don't underestimate the trust being placed in you. Any abuse whatsoever and you'll be back in solitary confinement with no privileges for three months. Understand?"

James was trusted with a tool bag and given a red armband, which allowed him to move freely throughout the prison without a warder. It didn't occur to him to abuse his position, he was pleased to be doing something useful.

After the first year, prisoners were allowed to receive one letter a month. James received his first letter at the end of February 1919; it was from his younger sister Mary informing him that his mother was seriously ill. The news shook James to the core and, for the first time, his faith was also shaken. He spent a couple of sleepless nights poring over his Bible by the light of a small torch borrowed from the tool bag. He searched for a passage that would save him and give him the reassurance he desperately needed. In the small hours of the second night, he gave in and flung his beloved Bible to the floor.

"Why?" he said into the darkness of his cell. "Why have you done this? After everything I've done? I've lived my life true to your teachings. I've endured so much and still you see fit to punish me!"

A surge of rage washed over him and he lashed out with his foot, catching a leg of the small table next to his bunk, tipping it over. The clatter reverberated in the stillness of the night and brought footsteps to his cell door.

"Landers? What's going on in there?" An eye peered through peephole.

"Sorry Sir, I tripped".

"Back in bed Landers. Now".

"Sir". James slumped onto the bed, his rage dissolving into tears. He hadn't cried since he was 10 years old and the stinging heat of the tears surprised him. Pushing his face into the pillow, he wept as silently as possible.

By the time he had washed and shaved the next morning, James had made peace with God and mentally formed a schedule of Bible study to help him deal with the news of his mother's illness. He hoped to be released from prison some time later that year and would be prepared for whatever challenges were waiting for him in the outside world.

HOME OFFICE WORK SCHEMES

The high number of conscientious objectors languishing in prison, coupled with scandals arising from the harsh treatment of some COs, prompted the government to provide an alternative option for the absolutists. In the summer of 1916, the Brace Committee, named after the Under Secretary for the Home Department, William Brace, set up the Home Office Work Scheme and a central tribunal to consider whether imprisoned COs had a 'genuine' conscientious objection before offering them work of 'national importance'. Men who accepted the Home Office scheme were transferred to Section W of the army reserve, which meant they were effectively still soldiers, but free of military discipline and undertaking civilian work.

The scheme caused a rift in the NCF; many felt it was an attempt to divide the pacifist movement and that, by engaging with it, COs were aiding the government in prolonging the war. Fenner Brockway condemned the scheme as a 'form of slavery'. Others, like Clifford Allen, asserted that the NCF existed to defend a person's right to act according to their conscience. Allen argued that it did not serve the 'principle of freedom to judge others in terms of one's own commitments'.

The men who accepted a place on the scheme found themselves in the peculiarly difficult position of being seen as shirkers from both their national duty *and* their principles. The scheme also divided wider political opinion; the MP Philip Snowden, a committed supporter of conscientious objectors, saw it as 'the defeat of both the military machine and the Military Service Act', whereas the Joint Advisory Council of war resisters argued that it was merely a 'continuation of the same persecution it claimed to be ending'.

Under the Home Office Work Scheme, work camps were set up throughout the country, notably in Dartmoor, Wakefield and Dyce near Aberdeen. If COs agreed to take part in the Work Scheme, they could expect more freedom than in prison and a small wage for a job that was deemed to be of national importance, but in no way contributed to the furtherance of the war. Or at least, that's what they were promised.

The government benefited from the venture by securing cheap labour for schemes supposedly run like businesses and returning a small profit on their investment. The work varied, but included quarrying, making fertiliser and sewing mail-bags, though the COs involved struggled to see the national importance attached to sewing mailbags for 10 hours a day.

In practice the work schemes were troublesome right from the start. They were often poorly organised, unprofitable and unpopular with their local communities, who saw 'slackers' living a relatively easy life while their loved ones were away fighting. In some of the camps, the men themselves grew restless; there were arguments and in-fighting between those holding different political beliefs and others, frustrated by the pointlessness of the work they were expected to do, simply gave up, walked out and were sent back to prison.

Dyce Camp was one of the most notorious work camps in the Home Office scheme. Opened in August 1916, Dyce Camp was situated in a disused granite quarry six miles from Aberdeen and about two miles from the nearest village. The 250 odd men who worked here were occupied with fetching large pieces of granite from the quarry in wheelbarrows, breaking them down by hand and riddling them to separate the usable rock from the dust and chips. The men were told that the rock was to be used in the construction of civil roads, but COs were used to questioning what they were told and one Saturday afternoon two of them followed a truckload of rocks on their bikes as it left the quarry. They were angered to find it being used in the construction of a road to a new aerodrome. This revelation led to a great debate among the men, who voted on whether or not to continue with the work. Surprisingly, only one man felt strongly enough to protest; Bert Brocklesby left the camp and went home to Yorkshire, where he was subsequently arrested and sent back to prison.

The future prime minister Ramsay MacDonald, still an MP at the time, visited the camp towards the end of August and subsequently described it to the House of Commons. He asked the House to picture a hillside with a huge quarry dump at the top of it. At the foot of the quarry dump there were pitched rows of tents where the men were living, exposed to the elements. When MacDonald visited, it had been raining for days on end and he was horrified by the men's living conditions. He walked the few miles from the railway station to the quarry and described the roads as 'huge swaying masses of mud', churned up by the heavy vehicles travelling to and from the quarry. Where the men were billeted the ground was half mud, half water and there was mud in the tents; the men were habitually damp and their beds lay on mud.

One of the main things MacDonald noticed was that the men were completely unsuited to the kind of heavy, manual work they were being expected to do. In civilian life, many of them had been clerks, teachers, shop owners and so on with the physique to match, which had subsequently been weakened by the rigours of prison life. The whole camp was badly organised and the work poorly managed; the men were frustrated and un-productive. A popular counter-argument to the complaints about living conditions was that if the brave men fighting at the Front lived in appalling conditions, why should these men be treated any better? MacDonald's response was that these men were exempted from military service and were supposed to be engaged in work of 'national importance'; instead, they were simply being punished.

Walter Roberts arrived at Dyce Camp in mid-August, having agreed to take part in the Home Office Work Scheme as an alternative to prison. Like many of the other men who had come straight to Dyce from prison, Walter was debilitated and ill-prepared for the hours of hard labour ahead of him. Despite his stoicism, he began to struggle both physically and mentally when the weather took a turn for the worse. When the rain came, it turned the land around the quarry to sludge; the men worked doggedly in the rain for 10 hours, before returning to wet tents and wet beds.

On 27 August 1916, Walter sat down to write one of his regular letters home to his mother. Perched on the edge of his bed, he shivered as he rested notepaper on a book and began to write.

"Stone me! I swear it's raining harder than ever!" Bartle Wild exclaimed as he pushed his way into the tent and hastily sealed the flap up behind him. Despite having his overcoat collar turned up and his cap pulled firmly down, his hair and face were still dripping wet. He began to take his coat off to cries of annoyance from the two nearest men.

"Hi! Watch who you're spraying water at will you?"

"Sorry chaps", Bartle said, easing the coat off more carefully. "Now, where shall I hang it to dry? Is there room left in the airing cupboard do you think?" His humour raised a ripple of grim laughter. He hung it instead from one of the many nails hammered into the tent posts; although there was no hope of it drying out, the excess water would at least run off it. Picking his way across the muddy floor to his own bunk, he reached down and felt the bedding.

"Still damp. Damper, in fact".

"Looks like we'll be back in the barn again tonight", Walter said.

"Fat lot of sleep we'll get there, lying on a hard floor and rolled up in a groundsheet", Bartle grumbled. "I'd give anything for a hot bath right now".

The men decamped to the old barn again, but this time they were ordered back to their tents. The order caused uproar, though most of the men had neither the strength nor the willpower to face up to any kind of punishment and, consequently, they did as they were told. By this time, many of them had coughs or colds and were beginning to feel like giving up. Ironically though, it was their poor physical state that prompted another act of defiance. Having been turned out of the barn and back to their tents, they were then ordered to work another 10-hour shift breaking rocks; they unanimously refused and wired the Home Office to complain about their living conditions.

By 31 August, the health of three men had deteriorated so much that they had to be separated from the rest of the camp and were billeted in an old ruin of a cottage on the edge of the camp.

"There're no frames in the windows, let alone glass", Walter told Bartle after he'd been to take some milk up to the men. "It's a wretched hole. Nowhere for sick men to be kept. One of the men is so ill, the doctor doesn't think it's safe to move him".

"It'll be a miracle if any of us get out of here alive", Bartle said, shaking his head. Then he added: "You know we managed to prop up our beds using the firewood?"

"Not much of a success, but at least it's lifted them out of the mud", Walter replied. "Maybe they'll start to dry out a bit".

"They won't you know. We were told to take the firewood out from under the beds and put it back in the woodpile. Only to be used for burning apparently".

"Oh for goodness sake!" Walter rolled his eyes. "Are they being deliberately cruel?"

Some of the men tried a similar exercise with rocks brought down from the quarry and the small piles of granite dotted around the camp were testament to their defiance when ordered to stop.

By the following Sunday, 3 September, Walter too had developed a chill. A few of the men from his tent had decided to walk down to the village for some fresh air and a change of scenery now the rain had stopped and Walter had intended to go with them. There was a tightness in his chest and a pain between his shoulder-blades; when he stood up he was assaulted by flashing lights and such light-headedness that he slumped back down onto his bed.

"I think I'm going to have to pass chaps", he said. "I feel dreadful. Not sure I'd make it as far as the village". As his friends set off on their walk, Walter climbed back into bed and tried to get warm.

By Tuesday, 5 September he was feeling much worse, having developed a fever and a cough which left him exhausted and breathless. The village doctor was sent for and after a rudimentary examination, a 'severe chill' was diagnosed. The doctor didn't think the condition was serious enough to warrant moving Walter into the hospital tent. "A few days' rest and you'll be right as rain. If you'll forgive the pun", he chuckled.

Medication to ease Walter's cough was dispensed and Bartle

Wild was charged with administering it.

The following day, while the men were all at work in the quarry and Walter was alone, he coughed so hard that he thought he was about to vomit. He reached for a glass of water on the night-stand, lost his balance and fell out of bed onto the muddy ground. He tried for several minutes to pull himself up back onto his bed but simply didn't have the strength. He called out for help and found his voice barely audible.

Walter remained lying in the mud until Bartle came back to check on him later in the afternoon. During those few hours Walter felt as though he were slipping in and out of consciousness; he saw his parents as clearly as if they were there in front of him. He thought of home: the smell of roasting beef on a Sunday morning; a long walk with his father as they discussed politics. He wanted to be back home more than anything on earth.

That evening, Walter decided to write to his mother. Any gap in his regular letters and she would worry about him. The problem was, he didn't have the strength to grip the pen firmly enough.

"I'll write it for you", Bartle said. "Tell me what you want to say and I'll write it. In my best hand, I promise. Don't want your mother to think you have illiterate friends".

Walter smiled weakly. "Thanks Bart", he said before giving some thought about how to begin; he had always been honest in his letters but was cautious of alarming his mother with the truth.

"Dearest Mother", he began. "It has only been a matter of time before the damp conditions here have got the better of me. Bartle Wild is writing for me as I am to weak too handle a pen. I don't want you to worry though, the doctor says it is only a severe chill. All the fellows here have been exceedingly kind and are giving me the best of care. I should be strong again in a day or two and will write personally. Your loving son, Walter".

The next day, Thursday, 7 September, the village doctor was called for again as Walter was now barely conscious and struggling to breathe. The doctor realised that his condition was far more serious than a severe chill and suspected pneumonia. He decided that Walter was too ill to be physically carried to the hospital tent and instead recommended that he remain in his own bed. The doctor arranged to call again the following day, when he would organise to have Walter moved by ambulance to the Royal Infirmary in Aberdeen.

Walter Roberts died of pneumonia on the morning of Friday, 8 September 1916, before either the doctor or the ambulance arrived.

Walter's death caused a national outrage and brought the conditions at Dyce Camp into the public eye. The government sent in the Scottish Medical Officer to inspect the camp and he concluded that 'the general sanitary conditions of the camp at Dyce may be regarded as satisfactory. The health of the men is not likely to suffer from living in camp, as long as the weather keeps dry'. But, he added, as winter was coming on, the men should be re-housed off the camp.

While deeply regretting Walter's death and offering his sympathies to the family, Under Secretary for the Home Department William Brace still did not believe that the conditions at Dyce were to blame. As he saw it, Walter's death was 'one of those unfortunate accidents that might arise anywhere'.

Dyce Camp's days were numbered; partly because of Walter's death, but also because it was fraught with so many problems. The men held a wide range of conflicting political and religious beliefs, leading to regular conflict and disruptions; they were wholly unsuited for the heavy nature of the work, unproductive, badly managed and frequently refused to co-operate. By the end of October 1916, Dyce Camp had been closed down.

The death of Walter Roberts also helped the NCF to reconcile the differences between those for and against alternative service and from November 1916 the NCF was prepared to offer its full support to the alternativists. Other work schemes continued with varying degrees of success and, all in all, 4,000 men accepted a place on a scheme as an alternative to prison. Most of the work camps suffered from some form of disruption because of the strong political views of the men. There were cases where part of the work-force would call a strike over conditions, while the rest continued to work; an angry stand-off would ensue and morale would plummet even further.

In early 1917, the Brace Committee was re-organised and attempted to run the camps under a stricter, military rule, which led to increasing anger on all sides. In November of that year, a more pragmatic approach was taken when the Home Office planned to release men who had served for 12 months with an exceptional record. The last work camps were closed in April 1919 and the Home Office Work Scheme was generally considered a failed experiment which had cost the lives of several men and presented the tax payer with a bill for £150,000. All in all, 73 COs died either as a direct result of their treatment, their living conditions or in some cases, suicide.

On the face of it, accepting an alternative to military service seemed like a sensible compromise for all but the most determined conscientious objectors. In reality, the men who joined the NCC found themselves in uniform and providing support for a war they didn't agree with. For some, it was a compromise they were willing to accept for many different reasons, but others felt unexpectedly trapped. The general public didn't respect them because they were 'having an easy time of it' and neither did other COs, who had stuck to their principles even in the face of imprisonment and dire hardship.

The COs who had originally taken an absolutist stance, but later accepted a place on a Home Office Work Scheme as an alternative to prison, were in a similar position. Despite steadfastly refusing to support the war effort, some 4,000 men could see no reason to refuse any work whatsoever and agreed to take part in work of 'national importance'. What they didn't expect was to be treated like convicts, given penal work to do for a minuscule wage and to live in accommodation not fit for human habitation.

Whichever option the COs took, they were punished and persecuted for upholding their beliefs.

CHAPTER 6

ABSOLUTISTS – COWARDICE & HYPOCRISY?

Absolutists – Cowardice and Hypocrisy?
(From a speech by Asquith to Parliament, June 1916)

In the public eye, the absolutists were perhaps in the most difficult position of all. The men who joined the Friends Ambulance Unit could be seen to be demonstrating bravery and moral fibre and those who joined the Non-Combatant Corps were contributing to the war in a practical sense, but what redeemed the absolutists? These men would not patch up injured soldiers and send them back to fight; they would not contemplate being involved in the manufacture of munitions or kit, the shipping of supplies, the digging of trenches or *anything* that might potentially assist the war effort. For them, even the donning of a military uniform and following of orders compromised their conscience.

If a man objected to military service on the grounds of his religious beliefs, there was sometimes a degree of sympathy for him. The tribunals, which included local dignitaries, magistrates and so on, might not grant total exemption from military service, but they could at least attempt to understand the grounds of the objection. If a man objected because of his political beliefs however, there was no sympathy and very little understanding; the country was at war and there was no place for a man's personal politics.

Those who could successfully demonstrate that their beliefs were longstanding and sincerely held may have been granted a partial exemption and drafted into the Non-Combatant Corps, but ironically, political objections to war were usually absolute objections to all warfare in any guise. This went further than just objecting to the killing of one's fellow man, it was also an objection to contributing to the war in any way. This stance, for either religious or political reasons, became known as 'absolutist'.

As far as the army was concerned, if a conscripted man was not granted absolute exemption from military service, then he belonged to them and must toe the line like everyone else. Although Prime Minister Asquith had made provision for conscientious objection, in a statement to Parliament on 29 June 1916, he was equally wary of those who might have 'put forward objections...as a cloak to cover their indifference to the national call and who [were] therefore guilty of the double offence of cowardice and hypocrisy'. He was quite clear in expressing his belief that 'cowards' and 'hypocrites' should be treated with the 'utmost rigour'.

This elemental clash of ideologies led to some appalling cases of violence, bullying and worse, as the army set about trying to break the men who steadfastly refused to be broken.

ATTEMPTS TO BREAK AN ABSOLUTIST

George Beardsworth, 21, Trade Unionist from Blackburn

The case of George Beardsworth, a socialist and prominent trade union man, is a stark example of what happened to many who took an absolutist stance. When George objected to military service on the grounds that the war was incompatible with his political, socialist beliefs, like so many in his position he was denied exemption from military service at a local tribunal. George's views were so strong however, that he had no intention of contributing to the war in any degree and that included following basic military instruction.

The standard military punishment for insubordination and refusal to obey orders was court martial, followed by a 28-day stint in prison, which George was prepared for. Yet, when it came to dealing with conscientious objectors, the military didn't always follow the rule book. George was about to discover this when, towards the end of August 1916, he found himself at the barracks of the 3rd Battalion Cheshire Regiment in Birkenhead.

Upon his arrival at the barracks George, along with a dozen or so other COs, was issued with kit bag, mattress and blankets. When the order to right wheel, quick march was given, George did not respond.

"Leave him to me!" a corporal shouted and four men ran at George pushing the kit bag onto one shoulder, the blanket and mattress onto the other and yanking his arms up to hold them in place. In this position, George was forcibly marched across the road to Park Camp and led into the police tent, where he was released and the kit dropped to the ground. One of the corporals picked up the kit bag and hurled it at George, who staggered as the bag hit him full on, cutting his forehead.

In a bid to make George accept that he was in the army now, he was interviewed by the pay sergeant and asked where he would like his pay to be sent and so on.

"I can't answer that", George replied. "I refuse to follow any orders and I have no intention of accepting pay from the army".

Later that evening, the sergeant-major visited George in his tent and he took a more relaxed approach towards persuading the CO to obey orders.

"Alright lad?" the sergeant-major said in an almost fatherly way.

"Good evening", George replied politely, though making no attempt to stand.

"What's this all about then eh?" the sergeant-major continued. "This nonsense about not obeying orders".

"I object to the war and I want no part in it", George said simply.

"Well we know that, don't we? That's why you're here. No one's expecting you to kill anyone, but you have to contribute lad. It's only fair on all the brave lads who *are* fighting. You can't get away with doing nothing at all for King and country when there are other men dying for it".

George hung his head and made no reply; where was the point in repeating himself?

The sergeant-major sighed heavily.

"Look lad," he went on, impatience creeping into his tone. "I'm trying to help you out here. Do you know how many conchies we've had through this camp? Hundreds. And we've broken every one of 'em". He paused for effect before adding: "And we'll break you too, make no mistake of it".

George made no reply, determined to show he wasn't intimidated by the threat. After a moment, a thought occurred to him. "Will my wife be allowed in to see me?"

"Not very likely", the sergeant-major replied. "Though it'd be a crying shame for your wife to see you being kicked all over the park", he added, watching for George's reaction.

"I've heard all about the way conscientious objectors are treated in the park", George looked directly at the sergeant-major now. "I'm prepared for it, but it doesn't do much for the reputation of the British Army".

Later that evening, much to George's relief, his wife Lillian was allowed in to visit him. She had known George long enough to understand how firm his beliefs were and how futile it would be to persuade him otherwise, although she wished he would at least make life a little easier on himself.

"Where would be the harm", she chanced, "in following basic orders and digging ditches or whatever they expect you to do?" It was only a half-hearted attempt though; George's strength of character and tenacity were what she admired most about him. The sergeant-major came back into the tent and, trying to get at George by intimidating Lillian, he said menacingly:

"It's our job to make a soldier out of him Mrs Beardsworth and believe me, we will do it".

Before Lillian was allowed to leave the camp, the pay sergeant also tried to persuade her to encourage George to give in.

"It must be difficult for you", he sympathised, "with your husband here and no income. How are you supposed to manage? We're in such difficult times, your husband is being plain selfish. What sort of man would stand to his principles to the point of not being able to look after his own wife?" The pay sergeant shook his head despairingly. "If only he'd toe the line, he'd at least have the comfort of knowing you'd be provided for".

WHAT WILL
YOUR ANSWER BE

When your boy
asks you—

"FATHER,—WHAT
DID **YOU** DO
TO HELP WHEN
BRITAIN FOUGHT
FOR FREEDOM
IN 1915?"

ENLIST NOW

ve) Recruits queuing to enlist, August 1914.
w) Recruitment poster: 'What Will Your Answer Be?' (*Library of Congress*)

(Left to right): Recruitment posters: 'Who's Absent?'; 'Women of Britain say "GO!"'; 'Men of Britain, Will You Stand This?'; and a poster designed to humiliate men into enlisting 'Daddy, what did YOU do in the Great War?' *(Library of Congress)*

MILITARY SERVICE ACT
1916

EVERY UNMARRIED MAN
of
MILITARY AGE
Not excepted or exempted under this Act
CAN CHOOSE
ONE OF TWO COURSES:
(1) He can ENLIST AT ONCE and join the Colours without delay;
(2) He can ATTEST AT ONCE UNDER THE GROUP SYSTEM and be called up in due course with his Group.

If he does neither. a third course awaits him:
HE WILL BE DEEMED TO HAVE ENLISTED
under the Military Service Act
ON THURSDAY. MARCH 2ⁿᵈ.1916.
HE WILL BE PLACED IN THE RESERVE. AND BE CALLED UP IN HIS CLASS.
as the Military Authorities may determine.

MILITARY SERVICE ACT, 1916

Every man to whom the Act applies will on Thursday. March 2nd, be deemed to have enlisted for the period of the War unless he is excepted or exempt.

Any man who has adequate grounds for applying to a Local Tribunal for a
CERTIFICATE OF EXEMPTION UNDER THIS ACT
Must do so BEFORE
THURSDAY, MARCH 2

Why wait for the Act to apply to you?
Come now and join of your own free will.
You can at once put your claim for exemption from being called up before a Local Tribunal if you wish.

ATTEST NOW

A.FENNER BROCKWAY
3607·11

ve l-r): Military Service Act 1916; 'Attest Now'; conscientious objectors had to apply for exemption before ch 2, 1916.
w l-r) Fenner Brockway, Founder of the No Conscription Fellowship *(Library of Congress)*; Clifford Allen, ounder of the No Conscription Fellowship.

THE CONSCIENTIOUS OBJECTOR
AT THE FRONT!

OH, YOU NAUGHTY UNKIND GERMAN —
REALLY, IF YOU DON'T DESIST
I'LL FORGET I'VE GOT A CONSCIENCE,
AND I'LL SMACK YOU ON THE WRIST!

WHY I AM A
CONSCIENTIOUS
OBJECTOR

Being Answers to the Tribunal Catechism

BY WALTER AYLES
A. FENNER BROCKWAY
A. BARRATT BROWN
CLEMENT BUNDOCK
J. H. HUDSON, R. O. MEN-
NELL & HUBERT PEET

Price Threepence

THE NO-CONSCRIPTION FELLOWSHIP
5 YORK BUILDINGS
ADELPHI
W.C.

Beken

H.M. HOSPITAL SHIP *GLENART CASTLE*. FORMERLY *GALICIAN*
Torpedoed and sunk, 1918

(Above left) 'The Conscientious Objector at the Front': Cartoon portraying COs as cowardly and effeminat
(Above right) Advice pamphlet published by the NCF to help conscientious objectors prepare for their
tribunal hearings.
(Below) HMHS *Glenart Castle*: The hospital ship that David Blelloch and Charles Dingle served on with th
Friends Ambulance Unit.

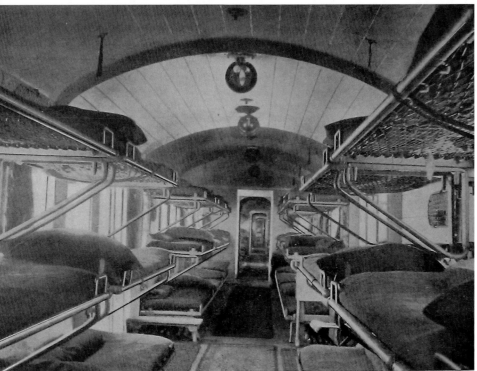

ve) Friends Ambulance Unit Train & Crew.
w) Lying Ward on AT17, Charles Dingle's train.

Name DINGLE Charles Fredk.

Married—Single 1|2|710

Address 68 Hill Lane Southampton

Normal Occupation just out of College.

Connection with Friends Baptist

Next of Kin—Name F. C. Dingle (mother)

Date of Birth 24 Sep. 18.

" " Address 68 Hill Lane Southampton.

Date of joining F. A. U. Aug. 19- 1916.

For, Amb.: Gen. Service: Agr.

TRANSFERS		PRESENT SERVICE				Exemption
Date	Service	Date	Unit	Date	Unit	Letter from War Office 5/6/17
		19/8/16	J.8	4/2/19	Left France	5 D.R./obj//183. CFD. will not be called up while serving with F.A.U.
		2/9/16	9 C.		Demobilised	unless point is raised by Tribunal.
		28.4.17	Wet. Aust			
		18/7/17	J. Agric.			
		10/8/17	Dunkirk			
		15/8/7	A.T.17			

Date of Leaving F. A. U.

Cause

L.T.&N

(Above left) Charles Dingle *(© Religious Society of Friends in Britain)*
(Above right) Walter Roberts, taken at the time of his tribunal *(Courtesy of the Peace Pledge Union)*
(Bottom) Charles Dingle's Record Card *(© Religious Society of Friends in Britain)*

(above left) Non-Combatant Corps badge.
(above right) Conscientious Objector in Non-Combatant Corps Uniform.
(below) Some of the 'Harwich Frenchmen': Jack Foister is second from left on the front row. Photograph taken at
Camp. *(Courtesy of the Peace Pledge Union)*

THE TRIBUNAL.

34 DEATH SENTENCES IN FRANCE

COMMUTED TO TEN YEARS' PENAL SERVITUDE

MR. TENNANT STILL HELPLESS

CONSCIENTIOUS OBJECTORS TO MILITARY SERVICE

TO ALL
THOSE WHO HAVE
ESTABLISHED AND
ARE MAINTAINING
THE RIGHT TO
REFUSE TO KILL

Their foresight and
courage give us hope

TO COMMEMORATE MEN & WOMEN ALL OVER THE WORLD & IN EVERY AGE

THIS STONE WAS DEDICATED ON 15 MAY 1994
INTERNATIONAL CONSCIENTIOUS OBJECTORS DAY

(Above left) Representation of Field Punishment No1: this was often used to punish COs who refused to obey orders once in the army.
(Above right) Report of death sentences for COs in France in *The Tribunal*, published in June 1916.
(Below) Conscientious Objectors memorial, Tavistock Square, London. *(Photograph by K. Burnham).*

The stand-off between the conscientious objectors and the army continued for several days with each man in turn refusing to co-operate in any way. One of George's friends, Charles Dukes, was taken over to Birkenhead Park on 22 August and put well and truly through his paces by the gymnasium instructor. He returned to the camp exhausted, bloodied, badly bruised and in a great deal of pain. George knew it would only be a matter of time before it was his turn and on the morning of 31 August, his ordeal began.

Birkenhead Park was the first publicly funded civil park in Britain; designed by Joseph Paxton and opened in 1847, is a large, landscaped area said to have influenced the subsequent planning for Central Park in New York. It was in this public park that the Cheshire Regiment had a parade ground and training area.

Forcibly led on to the parade ground, George was expected to drill with the rest, but again he refused to follow any orders at all. When he failed to mark time, two soldiers kicked first one leg, then another repeatedly, effectively forcing him to mark time. When the order 'eyes right' was given, he was punched in the side of the head and his head twisted round to the right. Throughout the morning George was made to run round the field, and punched continually if he showed signs of stopping.

This was all done in full view of the public, most of whom patriotically enjoyed watching the soldiers training, but some of whom must also have relished seeing the conchies get what was coming to them.

With the morning drill over, George was taken to the medical officer for vaccination. Despite having spent the last couple of hours being kicked and punched around the park for insubordination, George's spirit was far from broken; he refused to be vaccinated.

"Come on lad, don't be stupid", the medical officer hissed. "Why make your life any harder than it is?"

It was no use. George steadfastly refused and was led back over to the park, where he was handed over to a gym instructor. It takes a particular kind of man to be an army gym instructor and we can only assume by what followed, that this man was the worst of his kind and took a grim pleasure in trying to break George. After his refusal to jump over the vaulting horse, four men lifted George and hurled him over it; they then ran him headlong towards the water jump and pushed him down into it.

"Make him do it again!" barked Captain Mills, one of the officers overseeing the training that day. Soaking wet, dazed and in pain, George lost count of how many times this was repeated before he was taken to an 8ft high wooden hoarding.

"Are you going to climb it?" one of the soldiers asked. George, gasping for breath, barely had time to shake his head before they grabbed his arms and legs and threw him over the hoarding to two men waiting to 'catch' him on the other side. This was repeated a couple of times before George was allowed to rest, though not sit down. As he leaned his back against the hoarding, he heard the gym instructor call to the other soldiers training that day:

"Come along and see what kind of cowardly bastard this man is! Willing to stand by and let you lot do all the fighting for him".

As George looked up, he winced as he caught sight of, not only his wife Lillian, but also his sister, standing at the edge of the training ground. He could put up with most things, but being beaten and humiliated in front of his family was almost too much to bear.

George's memory of events becomes understandably hazy after this, though he does remember being rolled up a wooden incline and pushed over the edge, a drop of about six feet; being repeatedly run up a slope, thrown over railings and run down the other side again. He also recalls lying on his back with the foot of a man in his stomach, while others forced his arms and legs into a 'drilling' motion.

Finally, after being kicked and punched around the park a few more times, he was approached on horseback by Major Roddy.

"You claim to have a conscientious objection, but not on any religious grounds", the major said, looking down at the sorry state that was George Beardsworth. "I simply do not understand your position".

George made an attempt to stand up straight and look the major in the eye. "I am in no fit condition to either argue or explain my position to you".

The major shook his head. "You might at least take part in some physical exercises".

When George refused, the major shrugged and simply said "Carry on" to the gym instructor before riding away. George was subjected to a further round of manhandling and beating that day and again on the next, despite, by this stage, being badly cut, bruised and barely able to stand unsupported.

The treatment of Beardsworth and Dukes did not go unnoticed; in fact questions were asked in Parliament about their cases. On 18 October 1916, the Secretary of State for War was asked whether he was aware of the 'inhuman barbarities' inflicted on the men of the 3rd Battalion Cheshire Regiment in Birkenhead Park and was he aware that the men's legal right to a court martial hearing had been ignored by the military? Hansard further records that two of the men responsible for the violent treatment of Charles Dukes were so appalled by what they were being ordered to do, that they refused to repeat the treatment on George Beardsworth and were punished with seven days' confinement to barracks. The MP Henry Forster, Financial Under Secretary to the War Office, admitted that the 'irregularities' in the treatment of conscientious objectors by the 3rd Cheshires had been reported and the order for this to cease immediately had been sent via telegram by the General Officer Commanding-in-Chief, Western Command.

Contemporary newspapers report that four of the non-commissioned officers involved in beating Dukes and Beardsworth were brought before a court martial; the account of the court proceedings gives a fascinating insight into attitudes towards conscientious objectors. For a start, neither Dukes nor Beardsworth were prepared to give evidence against the men accused of beating them. It's possible that this is nothing more than a reflection of their absolute refusal to take part in military proceedings, or perhaps they blamed not the NCOs, but the whole military machine and its representatives, officers like Captain Marshall and Major Roddy. The NCOs had little option but to follow orders or face punishment themselves.

Eight civilian witnesses present in Birkenhead Park on the dates in question, were called to give evidence; two refused to attend and the testimonies of the remaining six varied. Some were prepared to admit that they had seen four soldiers being ordered to force Beardsworth around the course, shoving him off a wooden incline, throwing him over railings and generally ill-treating him, but were unable to identify any of the men involved. Others swore they had observed no ill-treatment whatsoever and that the NCOs were only using necessary force to persuade a recalcitrant soldier around the course, causing no apparent harm to the soldier concerned. Even a local policeman, Sergeant Hackton, swore he'd seen the whole incident and Beardsworth had not been ill-treated, he had not been in a state of exhaustion and bleeding from the face.

Lillian Beardsworth, it seems, was alone in speaking out about the treatment of her husband and others in Birkenhead Park in August 1916, but her testimony was simply not evidence enough to convict anyone. All four NCOs pleaded not guilty to the charge of ill-treating a soldier and, with the lack of corroborating witness statements, it was difficult to pursue a case against them. All four were discharged.

There is enough evidence surrounding the case of George Beardsworth to leave little doubt that conscientious objectors drafted into the 3rd Cheshires fell foul of military prejudice; it happened in a public park for all to see. Although the government acted swiftly to bring the army back into line and although the army subsequently court-martialled the NCOs involved, these were not isolated incidents. The reluctance of witnesses to identify the accused NCOs, or even to give evidence at all, suggests a general feeling that the conchies were getting no more than they deserved.

George Beardsworth's story is just one of many. Men who were refused exemption from military service on grounds of conscience immediately belonged to the army and if they refused to obey orders, standard practice was court martial followed by 28 days imprisonment. Released from prison, they returned to the army and went through the whole charade again.

For a small group of men though, the army took a different approach; one they believed would set an example so severe that it would discourage the whole notion of conscientious objection and get men to where they were needed the most: at the Front.

The 'Frenchmen'

Jack Foister

Jack Foister was a young man caught up in what was to become one of the most shocking and notorious episodes in the story of First World War conscientious objection.

Having had his application for absolute exemption to military service refused, Jack was expected to join the army on 23 May 1916. As he had no intention of joining any kind of military unit, Jack appealed against the decision but also knew that he was likely to be arrested when he didn't report for duty in May. Rather than cause any embarrassment to the school, Jack had left his teaching post and was waiting for events to take their course. What he didn't expect was to be arrested quite so soon.

On 25 April, nearly a whole month before he was due to report, Jack was arrested for desertion and brought before the magistrate in Cambridge, where he was found guilty of failing to abide by the laws of the land and sent to county prison to await military escort. While in prison, Jack received a letter advising that his appeal was in two days time. Because his application for exemption had not been resolved at appeal, Jack was actually under no obligation to the army and should have been released, but he was instead escorted to Landguard Fort, a military garrison in Felixstowe.

On arrival, Jack duly presented the letter which excused him from joining the army; he was released and allowed to travel back to Peterborough without escort. He lost his appeal and was sent back to Landguard, before being moved to Harwich Redoubt, an imposing edifice originally built to house French prisoners during the Napoleonic wars and now used as a military prison. Although still not officially in the army until May 23, and with another appeal at county tribunal to go, Jack Foister was nevertheless a military prisoner and had to endure all the accompanying hardship that entailed.

A lot of men would have been outraged by the injustice of their situation; but it's clear from Jack's unpublished memoirs that he took it all on the chin. Prison life was by no means easy; the prisoners were kept busy and Jack approached his work with alacrity to the point of annoying his fellow prisoners. When instructed to scrub flagstones in the yard, another prisoner Alfred Evans could take no more.

"Foister, you need to cut your output by at least 99 per cent!" Evans hissed as he scrubbed alongside Jack.

"Eh?" Jack looked up, surprised.

"Do you have to work so bloody fast?" Evans said. "You're showing the rest of us up".

Jack looked back at his half cleaned flag. "I just like seeing a job well done. What's the point in working all day and having nothing to show for it?"

"And what's the point in rushing through it? They'll only give you another job to do".

Jack pushed his glasses back up the bridge of his nose. "I suppose you have a point", he said with a shrug and took up scrubbing again. Although he didn't have it in him to do a poor job, he scrubbed each flagstone for a full 15 minutes before moving to the next.

"That'll do", Evans laughed, slapping him on the back.

On 8 May, less than two weeks after his arrest, Jack was shipped out to France along with 16 of his peers from Harwich Redoubt. They had no advance warning and were not allowed to inform family or loved ones of their departure, although they were advised to write their wills. As they boarded the SS *Clementine*, a corporal in the Military Police wished them a cheery goodbye, adding: "You'll be pushing up daisies in no time!"

Hansard for this period makes gripping reading and it's clear with the benefit of history and hindsight that the army and Parliament had very different interpretations of the Military Service Act and its provisions for conscientious objectors. Numerous questions were asked on an almost daily basis by MPs about the treatment of COs. Parliament expected COs to be afforded the same rights as civilian prisoners, whereas the army considered them disobedient soldiers subject to military punishment. Questions about men being clapped in irons, fed on bread and water and locked in tiny, pitch-black cells were raised by MPs and readily refuted by Harold Tennant, the Under Secretary for War, among others.

When news began to filter through that a number of conscientious objectors had been covertly sent to France, Philip Snowden, the MP for Blackburn and prominent campaigner for the rights of conscientious objectors, asked whether the men had 'gone willingly; if not, what is going to be done with them in France...?' He also asked for further assurances that the military authorities abroad would adhere to the Military Services Act, which 'does not allow the infliction of the death penalty on conscientious objectors for refusal to obey military orders'.

Tennant's reply, rather chillingly, suggests that Snowden misunderstands the Act, which states only that the death penalty cannot be inflicted in respect of a 'failure to obey an order calling up from the Reserve for permanent service a man deemed to be enlisted under the Act'. In other words, Tennant refused to rule out the possibility of the COs being sentenced to death for disobeying orders while in France. Snowden was understandably furious and accused the War Office of treating the government's promises as 'scraps of paper'.

Who was actually responsible for sending the COs to France is open to debate, but the man tasked with dealing with conscientious objectors, Assistant Adjutant-General Wyndham Childs, is likely to have played a pivotal role in the matter, particularly as he was also put in charge of army discipline that same year. Childs's memoirs record that he did have a little sympathy with conscientious objection on religious grounds, but none whatsoever for objection on moral, ethical or political grounds. Any letters complaining about ill treatment of COs while in detention barracks were to be 'ignored' and also his opinion that the No Conscription Fellowship should be tried under the Incitement to Mutiny Act.

Wyndham Childs was an army man through and through and had no truck with politicians arguing for the rights of conchies. As far as he was concerned, these men were in the army and if they didn't obey orders they would have to face the consequences. What made Childs a dangerous man was the fact that he kept his opinions very much to himself; publicly, he was the face of reason and friend to the NCF. When he gave assurances that no harm would befall the COs in France, he was believed.

In total, 34 men from various prisons and detention camps in Britain were shipped out to France in May 1916. They were unaware of the furore breaking out at home over their situation and, to begin with at least, unaware of the growing seriousness of their position.

Jack Foister recalls arriving at Le Harve on a 'beautiful spring morning' and spending his first few days at Cinder City, a huge encampment on former marshland which had been filled in with cinders and ash. The main inhabitants of Cinder City were recuperating soldiers who had 'done their bit'. Perhaps the army hoped that the soldiers who *had* fought would despise the COs enough to make their lives a misery and break their spirit. Ironically, the opposite happened and it would seem that some of the soldiers covertly admired the COs' strength of character. Jack recalls being impressed when on several occasions soldiers had wished the COs good luck and hoped they could beat the army, though adding: 'but nobody can'.

Foister and one of his fellow COs Jack Ring were marched onto the parade ground together, given orders to work and told that all the other COs were working. Of course Foister and Ring had no way of knowing whether this statement was true or not and faced the dilemma of whether to give in or refuse and potentially stand alone. They looked at one another and took a deep breath, before steadfastly refusing to obey and they consequently spent the night handcuffed in a cramped cell with seven other COs and a drunk. As part of their punishment their pay was to be stopped for three days, which made Jack laugh in spite of everything because he hadn't yet received any pay.

Jack was put to work in an engineering shop, but because the work contributed to the war effort, Jack would have no part in it. He stood beside the machinery for hours while others toiled around him; abused and berated, he still refused to give in. He was rewarded with Field Punishment (F.P.) Number One for his disobedience and moved to Harfleur along with his fellow COs.

F.P. No.1 was nicknamed 'crucifixion' because it involved the fettering of a man to a fixed object, such as a gun wheel, with his arms outstretched and legs together in the formation of a cross. The men were usually tied at a height where their feet only just touched the ground, so their arms took the bulk of their body weight.

F.P. No.1 lasted for two hours a day for a period of 28 days, with the remaining 22 hours of each day spent handcuffed in solitary confinement. Although life at Harfleur was undoubtedly arduous, Jack coped reasonably well and recalls F.P. No.1 as 'uncomfortable but bearable', whereas other COs understandably found the constant punishment thoroughly demoralising.

From Harfleur the men were moved to Field Punishment Barracks near Boulogne, where the punishment regime got steadily worse. F.P. No.1 now involved being spreadeagled and roped onto a barbed wire fence on the perimeter of the site, in full view of all passers-by. The men were tied up so tight that they had to take great care not to cut their faces on the wire when turning their heads. The majority of Jack's days were now spent in cramped, overcrowded cells with a single bucket acting as latrine for 12 men. Day in, day out, the men were sent out on parade and given orders which they refused to obey, then returned to the cells and given bread and water rations.

The men realised that something more sinister was afoot when a party of officers were admitted to the camp and Foister, Marten, Ring and Scullard were each presented in turn before them. When it was Jack's turn, he was told to stand in front of a desk behind which sat General de Gex and two other stony-faced officers. The officer to the left of General de Gex spoke first, his tone was quiet and level.

"Private Foister, in a moment, the General will give you an order. If you do not obey this order, you will be court-martialled for disobedience; the punishment for which could be the sentence of death".

Jack swallowed hard and thought back a couple of weeks to the moment when the fate of Gunner Summerhayes had been read out to them all on the parade ground. Summerhayes had been court-martialled for refusing to obey orders, found guilty and shot at dawn. Although Summerhayes had been on active service and was not a conscientious objector, Jack knew that his case had been used as a warning. Jack's predicament was clear: give in now or face a possible death sentence. Beads of sweat broke out under his collar and his throat went dry as he waited.

General de Gex gave an order to fall-in behind another soldier for drill, the order was as simple as that. Jack didn't move a muscle.

'Am I being a damn fool? Am I the only one?' he wondered. Drawing on every ounce of his resolve, Jack turned his back on the panel of officers and walked back to his cell.

As it happened, not one single man capitulated; each in turn found the courage to refuse the order and go back to their cell. Each man was subsequently issued with a charge sheet and the prisoners managed to find a grim humour in the wording of their crimes.

"An NCO heard General de Gex issue Private Foister with an order, Private Foister refused", Jack read out loud. "The accused said: 'I refuse or words to that effect'", Jack laughed. "I never said any such thing!"

"Apparently, I said the same thing", said Jack Ring. "Or words to that effect".

"Looking at the way mine's written", Howard Marten said. "It looks like I actually did say 'or words to that effect!'"

The phrase 'or words to that effect' was repeated so often throughout the charge sheets that it appeared ridiculous and the men began using it for the silliest of things. "Pass the salt old boy. Or words to that effect", they would joke, speaking in a faux upper-class accent, or "I'm off to the latrine, or words to that effect". Perhaps it was a form of protest, turning the undoubted gravity of their situation into a silly joke, or perhaps it was just a way of getting by while waiting for the army's next move; whatever it was, the men were determined to keep up their morale.

The date for their courts martial was set; the men were each given a sheet of blank paper and told to prepare their defences. Legally, they were entitled to a 'prisoner's friend' to represent them, though this rarely happened because few men in the barracks would associate themselves with a CO and the men weren't allowed to write home, so there was no way of having someone sent over from England to represent them. Part of Jack Foister's defence was that his second and final appeal against conscription had still not been heard and therefore he was not officially in the army at all. Howard Marten and a couple of others arranged for a cable to be sent to England on Jack's behalf, hoping to raise the alarm and have Jack sent home for his tribunal hearing. The cable was stopped by the censor.

Howard Marten was the first to go before the court martial,

the other men were lined up outside awaiting their turn. One of the officers overseeing the men shook his head and muttered, "It would be monstrous to shoot these men". Jack closed his eyes and thought: 'that's it, we're done for'.

Jack describes the court martial as something of a 'rigged affair', paying lip service to the appearance of justice. Each case took over an hour to hear, and all the evidence was presented before each man in turn was found guilty as charged.

On the afternoon of 17 June, the men were taken out to a parade ground packed with soldiers to hear their sentences. The adjutant read each man's sentence out in turn, beginning again with Howard Marten.

"Private Howard Marten...you have been found guilty of failing to obey military orders when on active service...tried by court martial and found guilty, you are hereby sentenced to death by shooting".

There was a dramatic pause filled with the heavy silence of a thousand men.

"Or words to that effect", Foister muttered to Jack Ring through the corner of his mouth; saying the first thing that came to mind to relieve the enormous tension. There were a couple of nervous sniggers which caused the second officer to glare at them, incredulous.

"Silence!" he hissed.

"If they shoot Quakers", Ring said to Foister, eyes still facing front, "you and I will be burnt at the stake".

Finally, the adjutant brought the pause to an end and continued: "This sentence has been confirmed by the Commander in Chief, but afterwards commuted by him to 10 years' penal servitude".

The men looked at one another in disbelief as each of them faced the same declaration of a death sentence being commuted to 10 years' penal servitude. The relief was dizzying; not only had they escaped with their lives, but they would be shipped back to England and a civilian prison. Over the next few days, all 34 men went through the same charade of hearing their death sentence announced and immediately commuted to ten years' penal servitude.

While this was happening in France, Harold Tennant, the Under

Secretary for War, was strenuously denying that anything of the kind was being carried out to a barrage of angry MPs. Question after question was being asked: had conscientious objectors been sent to France and if so, what was being done with them there? When were they being allowed to return?

On 22 June, five days after Jack Foister received his death sentence, Labour MP George Barnes asked Tennant to comment on reports that four conscientious objectors had been sentenced to death. Tennant replied that there had been a number of such rumours about treatment of COs, most of which were unsubstantiated and untrue. He even went as far as categorically denying any harsh treatment of the COs in France and claimed that there was 'no question of their being sentenced to death'.

Either Tennant was deliberately lying to the House, or he was genuinely unaware of events. A few days later he was forced to make the humiliating admission that 34 COs had indeed received the death sentence, but there is no record of an apology, despite accusations that he had misled the House. Asquith himself promised that no more conscientious objectors would be sent to France under any circumstances.

The story of the 'Frenchmen', as the 34 COs came to be known, is a dark and infamous episode in British military history. Shaming for the army and embarrassing for the government, the incident received wide press coverage at the time and even the sternest critics of conscientious objection could not condone the army's actions. No further COs whose beliefs were 'sincerely held', were sent to France. Instead conscientious objectors, who were not granted total exemption but took the absolutist stance, spent their days either in a civilian prison or as part of a Government Work Scheme, undertaking work of 'national importance'.

No man using conscientious objection as a 'cloak to cover their indifference to the national call' would have endured the treatment meted out to men like George Beardsworth and Jack Foister. Giving in to the army would have seemed the easier option to anyone hoping for a quiet life; it takes true courage and determination to stand by your principles in the face of such powerful opposition.

CHAPTER 7

ARMISTICE

At eleven o'clock this morning came to an end the cruellest
and most terrible War that has ever scourged mankind.
I hope we may say that thus, this fateful morning,
came to an end all wars.
(Lloyd George, 11 November 1918)

At the beginning of 1918, it had seemed as though the war would never end. 1917 had been particularly gruesome, culminating in the Passchendaele offensive, which started in July and continued until November, eventually costing the lives of some 250,000 Allied troops. On 17 December, an armistice between Russia and the Central Powers allowed Germany to move her troops from the Eastern Front across to the Western Front and, although the United States entered the war in April 1917, American troops were slow to mobilise and didn't see action until May 1918.

In March 1918, Germany launched the Spring Offensive that so affected Charles Dingle and managed to push the Allied lines back further than at any time during the previous two years. Sergeant-Major Richard Tobin of Hood Battalion recalled finding himself back in a trench they had taken from the Germans in November 1916.

So powerful was the German advance that on 11 April, Field Marshal Douglas Haig issued a Special Order of the Day to all ranks of the British Army in France and Flanders urging them to stand firm:

With our backs to the wall and believing in the justice of our cause, each one of us must fight on to the end. The safety of our homes and the Freedom of mankind alike depend upon the conduct of each one of us at this critical moment.

By the end of April, Germany had lost momentum and the offensive was all but over.

In Britain, the German offensive and resulting political storm threatened to split the Liberal Party in two, with Major-General Sir Frederick Maurice accusing the government of deliberately misrepresenting the number of troops being deployed to the Western Front. British munitions factories had worked flat-out to supply shells during the offensive and consequently, stocks were dangerously low, raising the potential of another shell crisis. The situation looked so bad that in April, the government extended the upper age limit for conscription to 51 and the Cabinet were making war plans for 1919 and even into 1920.

But the offensive had not been as successful for Germany as it might have at first appeared. Germany had gained ground but not victory, and where their forces had made advances on Allied lines, they had effectively created a greater area to defend at a time when German troops were exhausted and depleted. In the initial aftermath of the offensive, Britain didn't realise the strength of her position, particularly now she finally had the injection of American troops.

Life in Britain during that final year of war had changed beyond recognition from the patriotic excitement of the early days. The infrastructure of the country had evolved to suit the needs of a people at war, but it was beginning to crack under the strain. German U-boats were sinking one in four merchant ships bringing goods into Britain, sparking a real threat of food shortages. Compulsory rationing began in January 1918 and by April sugar, meat, butter and beer were all on ration. The rail network was buckling through lack of coal and sufficient manpower to maintain it and consequently services were regularly curtailed or cancelled.

In addition to everyday privations, there was also the undeniable human tragedy. Cities, towns, villages and factories had lost their men. There wasn't a corner of Britain left unaffected; a whole generation of men had gone forever and many of those who returned were fundamentally changed. Scarred, wounded, disabled or shell shocked, the men who came home couldn't fit easily back into their old lives.

During 1917, a new terror was visited on Britain in the form of the German Gotha and 'Giant' bombers; heavy, long range aircraft which could successfully bomb London and the South-East. In contrast to the half a dozen or so deaths caused by Zepplin raids, the new bombers could wreak havoc and easily kill 100 people or more at a time. By the time the war came to a close, the skies around London were punctuated by 50 miles or so of barrage balloons.

Throughout the summer of 1918, Allied troops managed to gain advantage after advantage over the beleaguered German troops and in August the German Army was forced all the way back to the Hindenberg Line, losing the ground they had gained in the spring. During October, the Allies stormed the Hindenberg Line, managing to break through at several points; finally it seemed that an end may be in sight.

On 9 November, with Germany unable to keep up the fight any longer and a revolution imminent, Kaiser Wilhelm III abdicated and escaped to Holland. At 5am on 11 November, an armistice was signed, which came into effect at 11am that day.

At 10.55am in London, Lloyd George emerged from 10 Downing Street to read a short statement:

At eleven o'clock this war will be over. We have won a great victory and we are entitled to a bit of shouting.

Five minutes later, at precisely 11am, Big Ben chimed for the first time since August 1914, as did every other church bell throughout the country. The nation erupted in raucous euphoria; there were impromptu parties and crowds danced in the streets. Stiff-upper-lip British reserve was forgotten and a kind of drunken abandon took over; celebrations stretched into the night under street lights bright for the first time in four years, and anyone in uniform was kissed.

Dense crowds gathered outside Buckingham Palace and chanted "We want the King!" until the King and Queen appeared on the balcony. The King made a short speech and the crowds sang the National Anthem, as well as contemporary songs like 'Tipperary'. Later that day, the King and Queen drove through London to the delight of enthusiastic crowds everywhere. The war was over and for now, that was all that mattered; no one gave a thought for tomorrow.

Reaction to the Armistice on the Front Lines of France and Belgium was a much more muted affair. Most of the ordinary fighting men had no idea an armistice had been signed until almost 11am and were still engaged in battle up to the very last minute. Major Keith Officer of the Australian Corps recalls how on one Front near Mons, the German machine guns were firing right up to the deadline, then a German officer blew his whistle and the firing suddenly ceased.

Many soldiers found the Armistice an anti-climax, too bewildered and exhausted to enjoy the moment. Corporal Haine of the 1st Battalion, Honourable Artillery Company remembers the men feeling so dazed that they didn't realise they could stand up straight without being shot at.

There were no celebrations, parties or drunkenness; just an eerie, unnatural quiet – something the men in the trenches were unaccustomed to. For them, it was a time of reflection and mixed emotions; knowing they should be happy, yet feeling sad as they remembered all the friends they had lost and the slaughter they had seen. Unlike their families at home, the soldiers did find themselves wondering 'What now?'

COMING HOME

The most obvious expectation among Britons at the end of the war was that life would gradually return to normal. Men would return home, to their civilian lives, families and jobs, and women, who had worked so competently in offices, factories and fields would willingly relinquish their new-found independence, return to their traditional roles of wife and mother and in time, normality would return.

Unfortunately, no one really understood exactly what normality was any more. Men didn't find it easy to slip back into civilian life and women weren't keen to give up four years of progressive independence. Returning soldiers struggled to adjust to peaceful domestic routines and most couldn't even begin to share their experiences with loved ones, preferring to bottle up their demons. Women tried to welcome back husbands and sweethearts they hadn't seen for months or years, often not able to reconcile the man before them with the man they had fallen in love with.

While the war was still raging, everyone had a common goal – defeat the Hun. It was simple and even those opposed to war understood what they were caught up in. When the war ended and all the rules changed, no one knew where they were heading or even how to begin.

The process of demobilising troops was a complex affair. Although the fighting was over, there was still work to be done, commitments to be met and wounded men to be repatriated. The initial plans for demobilisation set out by Lord Derby proposed that men with skills valuable to British industry should be released first. However, these men had been among the last to be called up and this often meant that men with the longest service were pushed to the back of the demob queue. The apparent unfairness of this scheme caused considerable unrest among soldiers desperate to return home so, when Winston Churchill became the new Secretary of State for War in January 1919, he made the demobilisation of troops his priority. Churchill devised a process based on age, length of service and number of times wounded, which generally ensured that the longest-serving men were released first.

Churchill was also the only one willing to tackle the issue of releasing conscientious objectors. Many felt that COs serving in the Non-Combatant Corps should wait until every other soldier had been demobbed before they were released. Why should the 'shirkers' and 'slackers' who had refused to fight be released sooner than soldiers? There were even instances of clerks involved in the dispersal of troops refusing to process the papers of men in the NCC.

The War Office ruled that any man serving with the NCC over

the age of 37 should be released immediately in keeping with the regular army; under that age, they must continue to serve. Some men remained with their units until 1920 and while the pay of regular soldiers almost doubled, the pay of men in the NCC remained the same. For the imprisoned absolutists, there seemed no hope of early release; they were expected to serve out their sentences regardless of whether the war was over or not.

However, there was a growing discontent with this continued persecution of COs and the NCF, the liberal press and some MPs began to protest over the insistence that COs remain in prison. It wasn't simply the issue of freedom for the men, but for as long as they were in prison their families would also continue to suffer; there would be neither pay nor pensions for families of imprisoned COs. The NCF set up a 'Set Them Free' campaign; 80 MPs signed and presented a petition to Lloyd George urging him to release all COs. The editor of *The Herald*, George Lansbury, presented another petition with 130,000 signatures to the Home Secretary. Finally, on 25 March 1919, 50 MPs of various parties adopted a resolution calling for the release of all imprisoned COs. This was the support Churchill needed to press forward and in April he persuaded the Cabinet that all COs should be released at the earliest opportunity.

On 7 April 1919, a statement by the War Office appeared in the *Daily News* which is so contradictory it is barely credible:

> *As a matter of fact the Army authorities themselves recognise that the lot of the conscientious objector is a hard one. They recognize that he has been the victim of ineptitude. Their view is that many hundreds of these men have been thrust into the Army whom the House of Commons never intended should be soldiers. The Tribunals, they consider, rejected the applications of hundreds of these men whose consciences were sincere, and to protect whom the conscience clause was expressly framed by the House of Commons. The Army did not want these men, and would have discharged them if it could.*

It seems that the War Office was admitting the persecution of thousands of men who held a sincere conscientious objection; men whom the conscience clause was explicitly designed to protect. This persecution, it suggests, was the fault, not of the government or the army, but of the local tribunals. Incredibly, the statement even goes as far as implying that both the government and the army were sympathetic to the plight of the conscientious objectors and had no choice but to abide by the decisions of 'inept' tribunals.

The day after this statement appeared in the press, the first absolutists were released from prison, although the Government still had no intention of releasing all COs at once. The first few were released because they had served at least two years of their sentences, while others were released on completion of their sentence or after two years, whichever came first. It was the end of July 1919 before Churchill was finally able to announce that all COs had been released.

Jack Foister

Jack Foister was among the first group of COs to be released that April. After returning from France facing 10 years' penal servitude, Jack had had an eventful few years. He chose to take part in the Home Office Work Scheme in the summer of 1916, spending a few months at Dyce Camp near Aberdeen, where the appalling conditions had contributed to the death of Walter Roberts. When Dyce Camp was closed down, Jack was moved to Wakefield Work Centre.

His mischievous sense of humour and disregard for rules ensured that he was no stranger to the authorities. Refusing to sign in and out of the camp earned him a black mark, bowling a turnip across the yard when he should have been working earned him another and a third came when he was found with a group of friends in his cell with the door shut.

These three black marks were enough to have Jack ejected from the work scheme and sent back to prison, first to Wandsworth, then Maidstone. Only allowed one letter every three months, Jack managed to sneak a letter out to his parents with a released prisoner, in which he devised a code for his parents so they could 'read between the lines' of his future correspondence.

At Maidstone, Jack was put in the printing shop; the work was absorbing, requiring some technical skill and Jack enjoyed his time there. He still objected to petty rules affecting his personal liberty, but on the whole he toed the line. He was in the printing shop one particular day in April 1919 when he heard his name being called from the doorway.

"Foister!" An unfamiliar warder stood in the doorway looking round the faces in the room for a response.

"Here sir", Jack said, partly raising his arm.

"Come with me", the warder said and stepped out of the room.

Jack's heart sank. 'Trouble again', he thought, as he hastened to follow the warder down the corridor. He'd flatly refused to have his hair cut and had been half-expecting punishment for it.

"Where are we going?" he asked the warder.

"You'll find out if you keep following won't you?" the warder replied, neither breaking his stride nor looking back.

Jack assumed they were heading for the punishment cells and was inwardly cursing about it; he'd expected a reprimand but this seemed a bit heavy handed. When the warder turned left instead of right, Jack felt a twinge of alarm – if not the punishment cells then where? When he realised they were heading towards the visiting area, a gnawing sense of panic set in; he wasn't due a visit for months. Had something awful happened to one of his parents?

As he entered the visiting room, he spotted his mother; she had her back to him and was reading the notices on the wall. As she heard the door, Jack's mother turned round with a broad smile spreading across her face. Her unlikely presence confused Jack and, as he stood in dazed silence, his mouth dropped open. His mother couldn't help laughing.

"You're coming home!" she said and laughed again, with tears pooling in her eyes. "At long last, you're coming home".

They hugged each other and Jack swallowed back a swell of boyish tears. It had come so suddenly, so unexpectedly that he had been wholly unprepared.

His mother had brought a small bag in which one of Jack's old suits was neatly folded. When he put it on and looked in the mirror, he realised just how much of a physical toll his experiences had taken on him. The waistband of the trousers was loose, the jacket hung off his shoulders and the shirt collar seemed to have a good inch to spare. He looked at the gaunt, bespectacled face peering back at him; his body may have been weakened, but his piercing blue eyes had as much energy and mischief as they'd ever had. He smiled at himself and said, "It's over".

For Jack Foister, as with all other COs released from prison, the legacy of his conscientious objection would hamper his integration back into society. In 1917, the government had added a sub-clause to the Representation of the People Bill, which denied the right to vote to any man who had failed to obey military orders on grounds of conscience. Effectively, all absolutists were disenfranchised for five years after the end of the war, unless they could prove that they had engaged in work of national importance or served with the Friends Ambulance Unit.

Logic dictated that if a man was not willing to fight for his country, then he should forfeit the right to take part in the selection of governance for that country. In practice however, the bill received a mixed response and was difficult to enforce. Conservative Lord Hugh Cecil argued that if deserters were entitled to vote, if fraudsters and robbers were entitled to vote, then it was absurd that men of good character, whose only crime was the rejection of violence, should be denied the right to vote. Jack Foister, unaware that it was actually a criminal offence, went ahead and voted anyway.

The biggest problem facing COs after the war was finding employment. It was hard enough for men returning from the army to find work, let alone those with the stamp of conscientious objection on their record. Jack was fortunate in many ways, as seeking work as a teacher meant he was moving in more liberal, enlightened circles, but even he was turned down by three separate headmasters. Despite his suitable qualifictions for the posts, the reply in each case was the same: the headmaster himself would be willing to take Jack on, but wouldn't dare fly in the face of public opinion. In the end, one of his old professors at Cambridge put Jack in touch with his headmaster brother, who offered him a position. After everything Jack had been though during the war, he took things in his stride and found it easier than most to settle down and get on with life.

Many COs released from prison were in no fit state to start looking for work, both physically and mentally weakened by the rigours of prison life. Even if they were ready, employers willing to take on a CO above a returning soldier were hard to come by. COs faced severe financial hardship in those early post-war years. The No Conscription Fellowship had considered this possibility as early as 1917 and had begun work to provide convalescence and training for COs upon release, also playing a part in the establishment of a Conscientious Objectors Employment Agency. With offices in both London and Manchester, the COEA was successful in finding work for 155 men by January of 1919.

Upon release from prison, a CO was provided with a letter detailing the help available to him and an address near to the prison where he could find immediate help if necessary. One such institution was Fairby Grange in Kent. Founded by Dr Alfred Salter, a Christian and pacifist who sympathised with the COs, Fairby Grange began as a convalescent home for COs released due to poor health. When the war ended, its scope was extended to provide not only medical care but rehabilitation for up to 30 COs. Salter was also chairman of a joint board created to provide relief and assistance for COs; within a year, the board received £9,775 in donations and spent £7,185 on direct relief, which included maintenance grants for 200 ex-prisoners and settling the accumulated debts of many others.

James Landers was released from prison on 18 June 1919 and returned home to Eccles to care for his mother. James was typical of the COs who found themselves in dire straits; there was no family money to help him, his mother and sister barely had enough to support themselves and he had no immediate prospects of finding an income. Signing on with the Eccles employment exchange, James began to look for work in earnest. He was a well-qualified man and as a trained electrician, work should have been easy to find, but many job adverts stated 'No COs need apply'.

"You're just going to have to lie", his sister Mary said one afternoon, when James had just spent a frustrating couple of hours first at the employment exchange, then calling in at several nearby factories. He was fully prepared to take unskilled labour if it meant earning a wage, but no employer was willing to take him on over a returning soldier.

"Lie?" James said, shocked at the suggestion. "I've just spent more than a year in prison rather than lie, do you really think I'm going to start now?"

"Having principles is fair enough, but principles won't put bread on the table will they?" Mary snapped. "They won't pay for mam's medicine will they?"

"Don't you dare lecture me!" James shouted, banging the kettle down on the stove. "I'm well aware of my obligations!" Surprising himself with the sudden flash of anger, he scratched the back of his head agitatedly. "I'm sorry. I can't bear being in this situation, not being able to provide and having to accept charity. I've never thought of myself as a proud man, but maybe I am. I've always taken pride in supporting mother, looking after her".

He pulled out a chair and sat down heavily. "I kept my spirits up in prison thinking everything would get better when the war was over and I was released. I didn't think it would be this difficult to find work. If I'm qualified for the job and a hard worker, why should it matter so much what I did in the war?"

"You can be so naïve sometimes", Mary sighed shaking her head. "Have you any idea how many men around here were killed? And most of those that came back aren't the same. You remember Bill Tanner?"

James nodded.

"Amiable, God fearing man before he went, give you the shirt off his back if you needed it. He's given to terrible rages now. No warning, he just flies off the handle and lashes out. Beaten his missus up more than once".

"Bill Tanner? I can't believe it".

"So you can hardly be surprised if people feel resentment towards you conchies when so many good men sacrificed so much. Feelings are running high".

James sank his head into his hands. "There must be some employers out there who understand, surely?"

He resolved to swallow his pride and apply for Out-Of-Work Donations from the employment exchange, to apply for any job at all that did not specifically exclude COs and not to mention his war record unless asked directly. In August 1919, James started work in a local factory as a bench-hand, only to be abruptly dismissed two weeks later, when his shift leader asked him which regiment he'd served in during the war. It was a bitter blow, because the longer he was without work, the harder it was to explain to a prospective employer, without lying, why he hadn't been working. In September, the same thing happened again, only this time he didn't even last two weeks.

On 11 November, 1919, exactly a year since the war had ended, James received a reply from the employment exchange about his request for financial help. The note, handwritten on an official Department of Employment form was brief and to the point:

Dear Sir,

I regret to inform you that it has not been possible to grant you any Out-Of-Work Donations for the period during which you signed at this Exchange on account of the nature of the discharge from HM Forces.

Yours faithfully...

So that was it. Because of his conscientious objection to war, James could obtain neither employment nor Out-Of-Work Donations.

Just when he thought things were never going to improve, one of his elder brothers, Philip, came to visit. Philip worked for the newly-formed British Dyestuffs Corporation Ltd in Manchester and knew the company was taking workers on. What's more, they were in need of electricians.

"You know I didn't agree with all that conchie business", Phillip said, "but I know you believed you were doing the right thing and you always strived to support mam when the rest of us thought she should be left to her own way of doing things. I've put in a word for you and they've agreed to give you an interview".

"Do they know I was a conscientious objector? I don't have to lie or anything?"

"No James", Phillip sighed heavily, "you don't have to lie. But I'd appreciate it if you didn't go quoting the Bible at them at every opportunity either. I have to work there too, and I've got a reputation to uphold".

James blushed furiously; his brother's attitude to the Christian Brethren had long been a bone of contention between them but, appreciating the help being offered, he did not respond. James went for the interview and was offered a job as electrician, a trade he remained in for the rest of his working life, though he was sacked a couple of times over the years for refusing to do something he considered morally wrong.

The post-war stories of the other men featured in this book are similar to the experiences of Jack Foister and James Landers. George Beardsworth, so brutally treated in Birkenhead Park, spent time in prison before joining a Home Office Work scheme in Dartmoor, where he was frequently at loggerheads with the various other political enclaves at the camp. After the war, George remained active in both the Trade Union movement and the Labour Party.

Charles Dingle stayed with AT17 until February 1919, before returning home to his family. Because of his service with the FAU, he encountered very little prejudice after the war and quickly settled into civilian life, as did David Blelloch. Both men were proud of the stance they had taken during the war and proud of the contribution they were able to make; neither regretted their choices.

It is nothing short of a tragedy that 73 COs, including Walter Roberts, died as a result of their treatment during the war. Ten men died while in prison, two drowned themselves, unable to cope with any more hardship (one had been sentenced to death in France along with Jack Foister and spent time in Dyce Camp). Another, C. J. Cobb, spent a total of three and a half years in prison and was only released at the beginning of March 1919, because he was in the advanced stages of consumption – he died three weeks later.

The sheer bloody-minded determination of the authorities to make these men pay for refusing to fight broke the spirits of many and caused the deaths of others. The courage of these men, who chose to fight for the principle of freedom and to defend the right of an individual to act according to their conscience, can never be underestimated.

THE COURAGE OF COWARDS

CHAPTER 8

POST-WAR CONSCIENTIOUS OBJECTION

War will exist until that distant day when the conscientious objector enjoys the same reputation and prestige that the warrior does today.
(John F. Kennedy, undated letter to navy friend)

Britain had long upheld the principle of personal liberty, but when faced with the gargantuan of modern global conflict, principles had to be compromised. The introduction of the Military Service Act in January of 1916 by Prime Minister Asquith was a landmark decision in twentieth century British history. Within this Act, however, the government recognised that while the majority of men would be willing to take up arms and fight for their country, the beliefs of some would make it impossible for them to harm or kill another man.

The decision to include a clause for conscientious objection to war was well ahead of its time and was lambasted by many as a get-out clause for cowards, shirkers and slackers. Despite being allowed by law, a conscientious objection was rarely understood by either the man on the street, the army or the tribunals created to judge its sincerity; even Asquith was wary of the conscience clause being used as a 'cloak for cowardice'.

By including a clause for conscientious objection in 1916, the government had, without realising it, laid the foundation for pacifism in Britain as we know it today. The experiences of Charles

111

Dingle, Jack Foister, James Landers, David Blelloch, George Beardsworth, Walter Roberts and thousands like them, were just the beginning of a long and difficult path, fraught with bigotry and misunderstanding.

Although pacifism can still polarise opinions, it is now a widely understood and respected position; no one wishing to stand by their principles would be subjected to the kind of condemnation and persecution meted out to conscientious objectors during the First World War.

In the years following 1918, the conflict was referred to as 'The Great War' and 'The War to end all Wars'. Most people believed that there could never be another conflict like it; that governments and nations would not allow such a catastrophic event to develop. In the 1920s, war memorials and cenotaphs began to appear in every town and village in Britain; for the first time there was a national compulsion to remember the war-dead as if perhaps, by keeping their memories alive, we could prevent it from happening again.

By the 1930s however, the international political situation was beginning to look precarious once more as the Nazi party gained power in Germany, and Spain descended into civil war. In February 1933, the Oxford Union proposed a motion: 'That this House will in no circumstance fight for its King and Country'. The motion was passed by 275 votes to 153 and was met with widespread criticism from the press and the government.

Winston Churchill referred to it as an 'abject, shameless, squalid avowal' and an anonymous critic sent a box of white feathers to the Oxford Union. *The Manchester Guardian* though, true to its pacifist principles, reported on 'youth's deep disgust with the way in which past wars for 'King and Country' have been made, and in which, they suspect, future wars may be made'.

Three weeks after the motion was passed, Winston Churchill's son Randolph proposed that it be deleted from the Union's records; he was defeated by 750 votes to 138 in a heated, angry debate and required a police escort to leave the building safely.

In October 1934, the Anglican priest and pacifist Dick Sheppard wrote a letter to *The Times* calling on the people of Britain to renounce war. *The Times* refused to print it, but once again *The*

Manchester Guardian took up the mantle and on 16 October published Dick Sheppard's letter calling war of any kind a 'denial of Christianity' and 'a crime against humanity'. Sheppard asked people to join him in renouncing war at a public demonstration and to send him a postcard pledging support; within a few weeks, he had received over 30,000 postcards.

The demonstration was held at the Albert Hall on 14 July 1935 and saw the founding of the Sheppard Peace Movement. In May of the following year, with the aid of George Lansbury, former Labour leader and editor of the *Daily Herald*, the Sheppard Peace Movement became the Peace Pledge Union. In 1937, Sheppard helped organise an 'alternative' Armistice Day service in Regent's Park for those who did not want to be associated with the militarism of the service at the Cenotaph in Whitehall.

By 1939 though, the threat from Nazi Germany was so great that Prime Minister Neville Chamberlain began to prepare for the worst. The Emergency Powers (Defence) Act put a framework in place allowing the call-up of military reservists and Air Raid Precautions volunteers, while the Military Training Act required all men aged 20 and 21 to undergo six months' military training. Nevertheless, when Britain declared war on Germany that September, this pre-emptive planning had produced just under 900,000 men; nowhere near enough to face the might of Hitler's army.

There was no option but to re-introduce conscription and the National Service (Armed Forces) Act was passed, making all men between the ages of 18 and 41 once again liable to conscription. In 1942, when it became apparent that the sheer scale of this conflict far outstripped the previous war, the scope of conscription was widened to include men up to the age of 51 and, for the first time, women.

The National Service Act, like the Military Service Act of the First World War, included exemptions to conscription and conscientious objection was among them. Neville Chamberlain had sat on COs' tribunal hearings in 1916 and understood the issues involved on both sides of the argument. Chamberlain recognised that it was impossible and unethical to try to force people into betraying their principles and so he allowed for three categories of conscientious objection: those who were prepared to accept non-combatant work with the army; those prepared to undertake work of 'national importance'; and those who would do nothing whatsoever to support the war – the absolutists.

During the Second World War, around 60,000 conscientious objectors were registered, including around 1,000 women. The tribunals set up to judge the sincerity of a conscientious objection were better organised than before: to avoid the possibility of coercion there was no military representative; the chairman was a county court judge; every panel had to include a trade union member; and, if the CO was a woman, a female tribunal member was required.

Around 2,800 men and 69 women were granted absolute exemption, 18,000 applications were turned down completely, and the remainder either took part in work of 'national importance' or joined the NCC, which was re-formed in 1940.

The government also took a more pragmatic view in supporting the rights of conscientious objectors, with the establishment of the Central Board for Conscientious Objectors in 1939. Fulfilling a similar role to NCF in the previous war and run largely by First World War COs, the CBCO had offices around the country responsible for offering help and advice to COs, monitoring the impartiality of tribunals and lobbying Parliament if necessary.

On the face of it, conscientious objection during the Second World War was a better understood and more widely accepted position than it had been 25 years previously. By allowing for absolute exemption and providing a robust process for dealing with issues pertaining to conscientious objection, the government was prepared to respect the rights of COs.

Unfortunately, this official magnanimity does not give the whole picture and COs were still considered by many as 'shirkers' and 'slackers'. There were reports of landlords refusing to carry out repair work on the houses of tenants who were COs; children of COs being bullied at school; and those COs who failed to persuade a tribunal of the sincerity of their objection sometimes found themselves trapped in a cycle of coercion and bullying.

In December 1939, Leslie Worth from Leeds had applied for absolute exemption from military service, which was denied at both local and regional tribunals. After refusing to attend a medical examination in June 1940, he was fined, compulsorily examined and conscripted into the NCC. Leslie failed to turn up, was arrested at the end of July, court-martialled and sentenced to 28 days' imprisonment on 17 August for refusing to obey orders. Released from prison on 13 September, Leslie was escorted to an Auxiliary Military Pioneer Corps (AMPC) unit in Dingle Vale near Liverpool.

At Dingle Vale Leslie, along with a dozen or so other COs, was treated with the same kind of brutality that had been the regular punishment of conscientious objection during the previous war. When the men at Dingle Vale refused to don a uniform, they were forcibly dressed amid a torrent of abuse. Rather than being charged with 'disobeying orders', they were charged instead with 'not complying with orders', a technicality which denied them the right to a court martial.

Put into solitary confinement, the men were shut up in cells 4ft wide, 10ft long and 10ft high, with no ventilation and a single blanket. They were fed on bread and water rations consisting of one piece of bread for breakfast, another for lunch and two for tea. For several nights in a row, they were woken at midnight, 2am and 4am to be marched around the parade ground in shirt-sleeves. Their heads were forcibly shaved and they were severely beaten by a provost sergeant for refusing to work.

Over the next couple of weeks the treatment worsened. Despite existing on four slices of bread a day and little sleep, they were forced to do hard drill, run around the drill-shed and jump over sandbags; shift piles of loose coal by the handful then fill sacks with coal and run with them. When they collapsed with exhaustion, buckets of water were thrown over them and they were kicked back to their feet. The men were repeatedly refused requests to see a major and for the right to a court martial.

The breaking point came in early October when, having refused to run round the drill-shed, the men were physically thrown from one non-commissioned officer (NCO) to another, with each NCO in turn punching, kicking or beating them with a stick, while second-in-command Captain Wright shouted encouragement. The men could take this for no more than half an hour before they gave in; one man had blood pouring from his nose, another had two black-eyes and all were covered in cuts and bruises.

Later that evening, the men were taken before the major and warned that they would be charged with mutiny for which the penalty was death. At this point, Leslie Worth and several other men agreed to 'be soldiers', and to comply with orders. Out of imminent danger, the men informed the CBCO of their treatment at AMPC Dingle Vale and an official inquiry was launched, resulting in the courts martial of both the officers and all the NCOs involved.

The case of the COs at the AMPC unit in Dingle Vale seems to have been the first of its kind during the Second World War and was raised in the House of Lords on 5 March 1941 by Lord Faringdon. Faringdon was seeking assurances that the War Office was rigorously ensuring that the law regarding conscientious objection was strictly observed and upheld the rights of COs. Lord Arnold commented that the War Office had been consistently 'courteous and helpful' in regard to COs and, although the Lords agreed that COs should 'suffer naturally under military law', they wanted to ensure that COs were not subjected to 'gross and harsh treatment'.

Conscription of women was a slightly different prospect. To begin with, only single women between the ages of 20 and 30 or childless widows were called up, though the scope was later widened to include women between 19 and 41. Conscripted women were offered a choice between military service in organisations such as the WRNS, the WAAF and the Air Transport Auxiliary or work in either industry or farming with the Women's Land Army. Women occupied many varied and vital roles from administration and clerical through to manning anti-aircraft guns and RADAR stations and delivering aircraft to RAF bases.

The last war had given women the vote, but this war provided women with the chance of independence and the opportunity to prove they were every bit as capable of undertaking demanding, technical and stressful jobs as their male counterparts.

For some women though, the issue was more complicated. Nora Page had been a pacifist and member of the PPU before the war and she had no intention of compromising her principles in the face of conscription. Although the National Service Act allowed for conscientious objection to military service, it did not allow for objection to compulsory industrial work or fire-watching duties, so Nora chose an absolutist position and refused to do anything she was ordered to do by the government. She refused to obey a 'direction of labour' order to work in a shop on the grounds that she objected to being ordered to do anything during the war that she would not have been ordered to do during peacetime.

Having joined a fire-watching team voluntarily, Nora later refused to register officially for fire-watching duties when it became compulsory, because the compulsion to register was an infringement of her civil liberties. It was this refusal that landed Nora in Holloway Prison for 14 days.

The experiences of women conscientious objectors in prison varied widely: some found the experience quite bearable and were well treated by prison staff; others were humiliated and abused, allowed one small piece of soap per month, one pair of stockings, no handkerchief, no coat and, unbelievably, no toilet paper. Throughout the war, around 1,000 women were registered as conscientious objectors and around 500 were imprisoned.

What of the men who had been conscientious objectors during the First World War? Many were now too old for conscription to be an issue, but some were not. The threat of Hitler's fascism was a very different prospect to the bumbling politics which had led Britain into the First World War and consequently prompted different responses from those who had previously objected to involvement in war.

Jack Foister, who had been prepared to face a death sentence in defence of his conscience, joined the Home Guard during the Second World War and followed orders so well that he had been promoted to lieutenant by the time the war was over. Yet, Alfred Evans, another of the 'Frenchmen', once again stuck to his principles, refused to register for fire-watching duties and wound up in Bedford Prison on Christmas Eve.

Another First World War absolutist, Howard Marten, was conscripted into the City of London Fire Guard, despite being in his fifties. He was unhappy about being conscripted, but felt strongly enough about the danger to London to relax his principles a little; avoiding fire drill as often as possible, but being there when necessary.

Maybe the very real threat of Britain being invaded by Hitler prompted some of the veteran COs to compromise their pacifist principles, or maybe because they were older now with families of their own, being involved in the defence of their home didn't seem too much of a compromise.

Even pacifist icon and founder of the NCF Fenner Brockway, struggled with the morals and ethics of pacifism during World War Two. A committed socialist, Brockway couldn't face the thought of fascism triumphing over socialism and knew he had to become involved in some way. Although he still identified himself as a pacifist, he realised that he could no longer justify the principle absolutely. So, while still campaigning for the rights of conscientious objectors, Brockway also became sector captain of a fire brigade.

Despite having served in the army during the First World War, the writer A. A. Milne was another prominent figure in the peace movement of the 1920s and 30s. In 1934, informed by his own experience of war, Milne wrote *Peace with Honour*, in which he argued that 'war is poison, and not...an over-strong, extremely unpleasant medicine'.

By 1940 however, Milne's views were so changed by the threat of Nazism that he published a response to his earlier work in the form of a 32-page pamphlet entitled *War with Honour*, stating that anyone reading *Peace with Honour* must now do so with 'that one word HITLER scrawled across every page'. He went on to argue:

Nazi rule is the foulest abomination with which mankind has ever been faced. I believe that if it is unresisted it will spread over and corrupt the whole world. I believe it is the duty of mankind to reject such a world. I see no way of doing this save by the use of force.

The face of pacifism was irrefutably changed by the pernicious threat of Hitler's Nazi regime.

Although National Service in Britain finally ended in 1960,

releasing young men from the obligation of serving their country, it still exists in many other countries around the world; some allow for conscientious objection, others do not. In Finland compulsory military service can last for up to a year and anyone refusing military service must do double the amount of alternative civilian service instead. Refusal to do civilian service results in imprisonment. Greece also has compulsory military service and did not recognise conscientious objection until 1997; even then COs were expected to do alternative service lasting up to seven times longer than the equivalent military service would have been.

Even peaceable Switzerland only passed a law allowing conscientious objection in 1992, but still severely restricts the grounds on which exemption can be claimed. One man registered as a CO in Switzerland in 1996 only to be called up anyway in 1999; his application for alternative service was denied. Refusing to join the military, he was imprisoned in conditions echoing those of the First World War: kept in solitary confinement, refused mail, sealed-up windows and restricted family visits.

Despite discontinuing the draft at the end of the Vietnam War in 1973, the USA still operates a Selective Service System requiring men between the ages of 18 and 25 to register so that a draft could be quickly arranged if needed. The USA allows conscientious objection on religious, moral or ethical grounds, but specifically excludes political grounds or objection to a particular conflict; so, if a citizen objected to the war in Iraq for example, he would not have sufficient grounds for exemption.

Although many countries now legally recognise conscientious objection, in most cases COs are expected to do longer alternative service or face imprisonment; either way, they are still effectively being punished for their principles.

British citizens are not required to take part in any form of national service, but serving soldiers in Britain today are legally entitled to an honourable discharge from the army as a conscientious objector. This might happen when a serviceman or woman is faced with being involved in a conflict they feel to be morally, ethically or politically wrong or which challenges their religious convictions. It is not an easy process and one that requires the objector to provide evidence of the sincerity of his or her convictions, but at least the option does exist.

As the world and warfare evolved so did the nature of pacifism and the motivation for conscientious objection. Some felt, and still feel today, that all warfare is wrong, regardless of the cause; others feel that some conflicts are inevitable because the threat from a particular government or regime cannot be settled by peaceful means. But fundamental to human liberty is the right to choose; to choose whether to join the military and face killing another human; to choose a non-aggressive role in support of one's country or to choose to abstain from any involvement in a conflict whatsoever.

The freedoms and rights we take for granted in Britain today have been hard-won over the last hundred years, and we should never underestimate the extreme courage of the men who chose to stand up for their right to personal liberty when their country was against them. The experiences of these men made subsequent governments recognise and accept the basic human right of the individual to act according to their conscience.

International Conscientious Objectors day is marked around the world on 15 May each year. In Britain, a ceremony is held at the Conscientious Objectors Commemorative stone in Tavistock Square, London, during which the names of some who 'maintained the right to refuse to kill' are read out. We should remember them.

BRIEF BIOGRAPHIES OF THE MEN FEATURED IN THIS BOOK

George Beardsworth
Born around 1895 in Blackburn, Lancashire. At the outbreak of war, George was an active member of the Independent Labour Party and by the time conscription was introduced, George was both newly-married and heavily involved with the Trade Union movement. His conscientious objection was on political grounds and he received short shrift at both his local and regional tribunals.

David Blelloch
Born in 1895, David won a scholarship to St John's College, Oxford in 1913, although he was unable to take up his place that year after contracting typhoid. When the war began in 1914, David considered applying for a commission but was still too weak from the effects of typhoid and took his place at Oxford instead. David found many friends who shared his socialist views at university and he began to actively campaign against conscription with the local branch of the No Conscription Fellowship.

Charles Dingle
Born in 1898 in Kingston, Jamaica, where Charles's father was a marine engineer. Charles spent his early years in Christ Hospital School, a boarding school in Sussex, before winning a scholarship to Taunton School. When the war started in 1914, Charles was 16 and an engineering student at Hartley College in Southampton (now Southampton University). Too young to enlist, Charles was pleased to be involved in the war effort when the engineering department switched to munitions manufacture. By the time he was old enough to enlist, Charles had developed a strong sense of pacifism and could not reconcile his religious faith with the demands of warfare.

Jack Foister
Born 1893 in Chesterton, Cambridgeshire. Jack's father was a boatbuilder at Pembroke College, Cambridge University. A

student at Cambridge when the war started, Jack initially wanted to leave university and enlist but was persuaded to finish his studies by his father. Jack's socialist beliefs led him to develop a pacifist stance during his final year at Cambridge and rather than enlist when he graduated, he found employment as a teacher.

James Landers
Born in 1893, James grew up in the slums of Salford with his mother. Much of his childhood was spent in and out of workhouses or living on the charity of reluctant relatives. By 1914, James was working as a bench hand at the Peel Conner Telephone Works in Salford and studying via correspondence course to become an electrician. James was a devout Christian and member of the Christian Brethren. Determined to live his life according to the teachings of the Bible, James had no intention of being part of the war but reluctantly joined the Non-Combatant Corps so he could continue to support his mother financially.

Walter Roberts
Born in 1897 in Cheshire, Walter was an only child. His father had been an active pacifist during the Boer War and had brought his son up to have a strong Christian faith and to believe that all wars were wrong. When conscription was introduced, Walter was studying to become an architect. An active member of the No Conscription Fellowship, he became one of the first conscientious objectors to appear before a tribunal. His charismatic personality attracted the attention of Fenner Brockway, founder of the NCF.

CONSCIENTIOUS OBJECTION – A TIMELINE OF EVENTS 1914-1919

4 August 1914 Britain declares war on Germany.

September 1914 The Society of Friends form a small voluntary aid unit, who begin training in practical field skills and general first aid at Jordans in Buckinghamshire.

October 1914 The No Conscription Fellowship is formed by Fenner Brockway and Clifford Allen.

31 October 1914 The Friends voluntary aid unit, now called the First Anglo-Belgian Ambulance Unit and comprising of 43 men, sets sail from Dover for Dunkirk.

June 1915 The First Anglo-Belgian Ambulance Unit, now known as the Friends Ambulance Unit (FAU) and has firmly established its role as a voluntary aid unit throughout Britain, France and Belgium.

July 1915 The National Registration Scheme in Britain, a kind of census, records the occupations of men and women aged 15 -65 years.

October 1915 The Derby Scheme: Based on the information gathered during the National Registration Scheme, all men of fighting are encouraged to 'attest', (i.e. promise to serve their country if called).

January 1916 Conscription is introduced: Every unmarried man between 18 and 41 years old is now 'deemed to have enlisted for the period of the war'. The clause includes exemption from military service for those men with a conscientious objection to war.

April 1916	First tribunal hearings of men claiming exemption from military service on grounds of conscientious objection.
May 1916	Thirty-four conscientious objectors are shipped secretly out to France, where they are deemed to be on active service.
June 1916	Conscientious objectors in France are delivered the death penalty.
August 1916	Dyce Work Camp opens near Aberdeen. Several other work centres also open at this time to provide conscientious objectors with work of 'national importance' as an alternative to prison.
11 November 1918	Armistice.
April 1919	First conscientious objectors released from prison: Those serving with the NCC or FAU remain with their units until their work is complete.

GLOSSARY OF TERMS

AT   Ambulance Train

CBCO   Central Board for Conscientious Objectors (WW2)

CCS   Casualty Clearing Station

COEA   Conscientious Objectors Employment Agency

FAU   Friends Ambulance Unit

F.P.   Field Punishment

ILP   Independent Labour Party

NCC   Non-Combatant Corps

NCF   No Conscription Fellowship

NCO   Non-Commissioned Officer

PPU   Peace Pledge Union

RAMC   Royal Army Medical Corps

BIBLIOGRAPHY

Arthur, Max, *Forgotten Voices Of The Great War*, (London: Random House, 2002).

Ayles, Walter; Brockway, Fenner et al, *Why I am a Conscientious Objector*, (London: The No Conscription Fellowship, 1916).

Bibbings, Lois S., *Telling Tales About Men*, (Manchester: Manchester University Press, 2009).

Bishop, Alan & Bostridge, Mark eds, *First World War Letters of Vera Brittain And Four Friends*, (London: Abacus, 1999).

Carpenter, Edward, *Never Again! A Protest And a Warning Addressed to the Peoples of Europe*, (Manchester: The National Labour Press Ltd, 1916).

Chapman, Guy, *Vain Glory*, (London: Cassell, 1968).

De-Groot, Gerald J., *Blighty: British Society in the Era of the Great War*, (Harlow: Addison Wesley Longman Ltd, 1996).

Ellsworth-Jones, Will, *We Will Not Fight: The Untold Story of the First World War's Conscientious Objectors*, (London: Aurum Press Ltd, 2008).

Goodall, Felicity, *A Question of Conscience*, (Stroud: Sutton Publishing, 1997).

Graham, John W., *Conscription and Conscience, A History 1916 -1919*, (London: George Allen & Unwin Ltd, 1922).

Gullace, Nicoletta F., 'White Feathers and Wounded Men: Female Patriotism and the Memory of the Great War. *The Journal of British Studies*, Vol. 36, No. 2, pp.178-206.

James, Stanley B., *The Men Who Dared*, (London: C. W. Daniel Ltd, 1917).

Kennedy, T. C., *The Hound of Conscience*, (Fayetteville: The University of Arkansas Press, 1981).

Kernahan, Coulson, *The Experiences of a Recruiting Officer,* (London: Hodder and Stoughton, 1915).

Milne, A. A., *Peace with Honour,* (London: Methuen, 1934).

Milne, A. A., *War with Honour,* (London: Macmillan War Pamphlet No 2, 1940).

Pearce, Goodall, 'Typical' Conscientious Objectors – A Better Class of Conscience? No Conscription Fellowship Image Management and the Manchester Contribution 1916-1918, *Manchester Region History Review.* Vol 17; 2004, pp.38-50.

Rubinstein, David, *York Friends and the Great War,* (York: Borthwick Institute of Historical Research, 1999).

Tatham, Maeburn and Miles, James E., ed, *The Friends Ambulance Unit 1914 – 1919: a record* (London: The Swarthmore Press Ltd, 1920).

Taylor, A. J. P, *How Wars Begin,* (London: Hamish Hamilton Ltd, 1979).

SOURCES

University of Leeds, Special Collections - Liddle Collection
(http://library.leeds.ac.uk/liddle-collection)

The Liddle Collection is a large resource consisting mainly of interviews with those involved in the First World War, along with diaries, letters, official documents and so on. The first-hand accounts within the collection archive formed the basis for much of my research, particularly for the personal stories of the conscientious objectors featured in this book.

The British Library
(www.bl.uk)

The British Library is an excellent source of obscure publications contemporary with the First World War ; in particular books such as *The Friends Ambulance Unit 1914 – 1919: a record* and pamphlets like *Never Again! A Protest And a Warning Addressed to the Peoples of Europe.*

Hansard Millbank Systems
(Hansard.millbanksystems.com. Sittings in the 20th Century. [online] Available at: http://hansard.millbanksystems.com/sittings/1910s)

An invaluable online resource for transcripts of sittings in the House of Commons and House of Lords.

The Friends House Library
The Library of the Religious Society of Friends in Britain
Friends House
173-177 Euston Road
London
NW1 2BJ
(www.quaker.org.uk/library)

The Peace Pledge Union
41b Brecknock Road
London N7 0BT
(www.ppu.org.uk)

INDEX

131